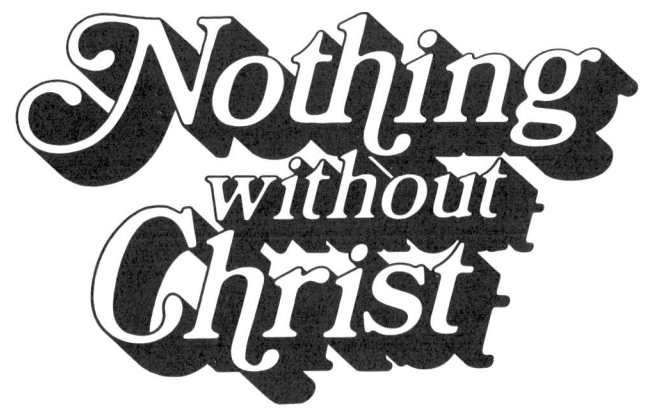

*Some current religious problems in the
light of seventeenth century thought and experience.*

DEAN FREIDAY

Published with the assistance
of the Rebecca White Trust

The Barclay Press
Newberg, Oregon

Dedication

To our son Will, our daughter Gail, her husband Bruce, their children Scott and Drew.

NOTHING WITHOUT CHRIST

© 1984 by Dean Freiday

All rights reserved. No part of this book may be reproduced in any form without permission from the copyright holder except brief quotes for a review.

ISBN 0-913342-44-0
Library of Congress Catalog Card Number: 84-70040

Printed in U.S.A. by
THE BARCLAY PRESS
A Concern of Friends
Newberg, Oregon 97132

Scripture quotations marked NEB are from the New English Bible, copyright © The Delegates of the Oxford University Press, and The Syndics of the Cambridge University Press 1961, 1970. Used by permission.

Scripture quotations marked TEV are from the Good News Bible: The Bible in Today's English Version, copyright 1976 by the American Bible Society. Used by permission.

Scripture quotations marked JB are from The Jerusalem Bible, copyright © 1966 by Darton, Longman & Todd, Ltd. and Doubleday & Company, Inc. Used by permission.

Scripture quotations marked RSV are from the Revised Standard Version of the Bible, copyright 1946, 1952, © 1971, 1973, Division of Christian Education, National Council of the Churches of Christ in the U.S.A. Used by permission.

Table of Contents

Foreword			vii
Preface			xi
Chapter	1	THE GOSPEL	1
Chapter	2	RIGHTEOUSNESS, HOLINESS, AND REGENERATION	7
Chapter	3	AUTHENTICITY, GENUINENESS, TRUTH	11
Chapter	4	THE CHURCH AND MINISTRY	17
Chapter	5	WORSHIP IN SPIRIT AND IN TRUTH	31
Chapter	6	ORDER	45
Chapter	7	SCRIPTURE	63
Chapter	8	THE TRIUNITY OF GOD	79
Chapter	9	MAKING ROOM FOR THE GRACE OF GOD	93
Chapter	10	BOTTOM-LINE CHRISTIANITY	101
Appendix	1	Catholicity and Quakerism	113
Appendix	2	A Discussion of Method and Some Conclusions	119

About the Title

One can find the basis for the title *Nothing Without Christ* in the writings of both William Penn and Robert Barclay. "I hope we shall ever remember," Penn states, "who it was that said, 'Of yourselves you can do nothing.'"[1] (John 15:5) Those who are His disciples "have learned by good experience, that without Christ they can do nothing."[2]

With perhaps a reminiscence of Romans 8:26-27, Robert Barclay adds, *[286]* "since we can do nothing without Christ, we cannot [even] pray without the concurrence and assistance of his Spirit."

Although the same wording does not seem to be in George Fox's works or writings, he does declare early in his *Journal*, "[I saw] that all was done and to be done in and by Christ."[3] "We are nothing, Christ *is all*."[4]

Italic figures in brackets within the text refer to page numbers in *Barclay's Apology in Modern English.*

1 Wm. Penn, *Works*, (London: Phillips, 1825) III:461.
2 Wm. Penn, *Works*, (1677), *loc. cit.* II:347, 390, 448.
3 George Fox, *Journal*, revised edition by John L. Nickalls (Cambridge: University Press, 1952), p. 14.
4 George Fox, *Journal*, revised edition by John L. Nickalls (Cambridge: University Press, 1952), p. 52, also George Fox, *Works of George Fox*, 8 vols. (Philadelphia: M.T.C. Gould, 1831) 6:356.

Acknowledgments

For a work that has developed gradually over a period of years it is difficult to know whose help and influence should be singled out for appreciation. After several attempts to do it in some other way, a listing of names in alphabetical order seems best: Lewis Benson, Wilmer Cooper, Maurice A. Creasey, Esther S. Freiday, Douglas Gwyn, Verlin O. Hinshaw, J. Calvin Keene, Mary Loretto, R.S.M., John McCandless, Lawrence McK. Miller, Donald S. Nesti, C.S.Sp., Arthur O. Roberts, Robert J. Rumsey, Douglas V. Steere. Errors and opinions, however, are mine.

While most of the research for this particular volume was done with the resources of my own library, Speer Library of Princeton Theological Seminary, so helpful with my earlier work, cheerfully provided supplemental material and staff assistance wherever these were needed.

Richard Eichenberger and others of the staff at Barclay Press gave more than routine attention to seeing the work through the press. —D. F.

Foreword

This book interprets the nature and significance of the seventeenth century Quaker awakening of the Church, and deals particularly with the Christ-centered theology of Robert Barclay as it relates to that of others who gave shape to that movement. The book not only gives evidence for, but is an aspect of, a recent scholarly reappraisal of what was normative in the early Quaker movement and its relevance for contemporary Christian issues.

Following World War II considerable theological reflection took place, within both Roman Catholic and Protestant churches. Vatican II called public attention to Roman Catholic reconstructions. Protestant reconstructions, although less visible, have been significant, and certain of these developments provide a useful context for understanding the present volume.

During the early part of this century Protestant thought had become polarized, with the terms "modernist" and "fundamentalist" appearing as labels for opposing systems. The orthodox Protestant center had failed to hold. After World War II, however, mediating theologies arose from each polarity. These theologies served to rebuild the center, a process that has continued until the present although the "new right" now threatens the equilibrium.

One of the moderating tendencies came from the "modernist" side. Sometimes dubbed "neo-orthodox" but more aptly understood as "neo-liberal," this movement helped the Church reemphasize (in contemporary terms) Christian doctrines of sin and grace. Theologians such as Emil Brunner, Karl Barth, and the brothers Niebuhr contributed much to this reconstruction.

From the "fundamentalist" side came a new thrust toward center. Sometimes referred to as "neo-evangelical," the movement helped conservative scholars recover tested hermeneutical principles for understanding the Bible, the authority of which constitutes a major point in their theology. Concomitantly, neo-evangelicalism brought about a renewed emphasis upon the Lordship of Christ and upon Kingdom ethics. Bernard Ramm, F. F. Bruce, Carl Henry, René Padílla, and Timothy Smith are some of the leaders of this movement.

One might say Bonhoeffer's indictment of "cheap grace" had challenged the superficialities along the whole theological spectrum.

Quakers were influenced by these movements, which served to reduce the polarities and to encourage a fresh look at the original seventeenth-century movement. Quakers were influenced, also, by the resurgence of Anabaptist scholarship under persons such as Guy Hershberger, Harold Bender, John Howard Yoder, and Myron Augsburger. Mennonite activism is sustained by an explicit biblical base, and has provided a corrective to the often less explicitly biblical activism of Friends. The New Call to Peacemaking, involving all groups of Friends as well as Mennonite and Brethren bodies, provided a forum for Quaker reconstruction of a theology of service. The process was not unilateral: Quakers contributed a methodology of involvement in political and social action. Through such dialogue Quakers have had to reevaluate their concepts of perfection, moving away from superficial political and superficial pietistic formulations.

Certain Quaker writers have served as catalysts to draw the polarities toward the center. Elfrida Vipont Foulds, Thomas Kelly, Elton Trueblood, and Richard Foster must be included in their number. Various renewal movements contributed, also, such as the Association of Evangelical Friends (1947-1970), with its conferences and papers, and the Quaker Theological Discussion Group, with its journal, *Quaker Religious Thought*, which is now in its twenty-fifth year. Emerging out of the important St. Louis Conference (1970), which drew from all segments of the Society of Friends, the Faith and Life movement contributed greatly both to the clarification of perspectives and to a recovery of normative Quakerism. This occurred through a series of conferences and through study booklets. The New Foundations movement has built upon the research, writing, and speaking of Lewis and Sarah Benson. Coming from the conservative side of nonpastoral Quakerdom, this movement has, nevertheless, appealed to persons across a wide spectrum of Quakerdom.

Earlham School of Religion came into being in 1960, impelled by the vision of Wilmer Cooper, its first dean. It has contributed greatly to the centralizing tendency in Quaker thought, particularly through its preparation of leaders for both pastoral and nonpastoral meetings. The Quaker colleges should not be overlooked in this respect, either. They continue to shape the future of Friends. A recent movement, the Friends Association of Higher Education, aims at increasing the Christian vitality of the colleges and also their fidelity to Quaker thought and practice.

For several of these movements the Friends World Committee for Consultation has served as an increasingly useful regional and world secretariat. Through its gatherings Quaker groups are kept in touch with each other. It is a forum for *koinonia*, at least, if not so much for *kerygma*.

What about the fruit from such vigorous branching and growing on the Quaker "tree"? Some fruit is yet to appear, but some is here. Consider the national pastors' conferences, the youth gatherings ("Youthquake"), editorial cooperation by the three major magazines, interyearly meeting visitation, broadened participation in regional and world conferences, and the emergence of younger scholars who are taking their places of leadership in the meetings and the schools.

Where are the roots for such renewal movements? In the post-war research (many of them doctoral studies) of a number of scholars, among whom are Maurice Creasey, Wilmer Cooper, T. Canby Jones, Hugh Barbour, Lewis Benson, and the present writer. These studies probed the radical Puritan context for the early Quaker renewal of the Church. They clearly moved away from Rufus Jones's heavy emphasis upon mysticism, following the lead of a mentor, Henry Cadbury. They also evidenced the influence of either neo-liberal or neo-evangelical Protestant reconstructions.

To this list of persons who dealt radically (at the roots) with the Quaker heritage – an admittedly incomplete list – must be added the author of this present volume, Dean Freiday. He stands outside of academia (like Lewis Benson) but not outside thorough scholarship. His careful studies of Robert Barclay resulted in the publication in 1967 of *Barclay's Apology in Modern English*. It has twice been reprinted to meet steady demand. Readers like the clarity of thought that comes from his bold "English to English" translation, and profit from the introductions and the thorough footnoting. Renewed interest in Robert Barclay by some of the scholars mentioned above, particularly Creasey and Freiday, prompted some reconsiderations (and theological recentering) by Elton Trueblood, who published a biography of Barclay in 1968.

This modern English version has had significant effect upon local meetings and churches. It has made accessible to contemporary Americans what was once a standard Quaker reference book. It is once again used in membership classes, or given to inquirers. It should be noted, additionally, that Dean Freiday has become knowledgeable of recent Roman Catholic scholarship and has been able to place Quaker thought in relationship with Catholic as well as Protestant theology. In fact, the "Catholic-Quaker dialogue" has yielded other results, for Catholic scholars have had their attention drawn to the Quaker understanding of significant theological issues. *Grace and Faith: the Means of Salvation*, is one of the publications arising from that dialogue. Written by Donald S. Nesti, C.S.Sp. with whom the dialogue originated, this analysis of early Quaker soteriology grew out of a dissertation submitted to the Gregorian University (Rome).

This present volume, *Nothing Without Christ*, is an excellent companion to Barclay's *Apology in Modern English* and provides a way into that volume as well as offering a deeper look at some of the theological presuppositions behind it. Issues central to Christian theology were raised by Robert Barclay in the seventeenth century that are central to the Church today. Among them are the meaning of the Gospel, the nature of ministry, the place of the Holy Spirit in relationship to Scripture and the Church, and the meaning of holiness. Because Barclay continues to be a major figure in the history of Christian thought, this interpretive volume by a leading Barclay scholar is received with appreciation.

—*Arthur O. Roberts*
George Fox College

Preface

Several ideas prompted the writing of this book. One was a profound sense of respect for the insights and capabilities of a group of seventeenth century religious thinkers. One's appreciation for their competence and the sophistication with which they dealt with major doctrines and problem areas of Christian thought grows as one broadens familiarity with their writings.

Although other names could be added to the half dozen treated here, these were preeminent: George Fox (1624-1691), without formal training, but the most creative of them all, and head and shoulders above most religious writers of seventeenth century England, especially in his perception of Scripture and his grasp of the sweep of Christian history. Robert Barclay (1648-1690), whose formal theological background was acquired under the tutelage of his uncle of the same name (c1612-1682), a priest and principal of the Roman Catholic Scots College in Paris. William Penn (1644-1718), son of Admiral Sir William Penn, who was a follower for a time of John Owen, the Congregationalist. Penn also studied at Saumur, a French Reformed seminary. Isaac Penington (1616-1679), son of Sir Isaac Penington (Puritan Lord Mayor of London), educated at Catherine Hall, Cambridge. George Keith (c1639-1716) M.A., Marischal College, Aberdeen, a Presbyterian minister before becoming a Quaker. Samuel Fisher (1605-1665) M.A., Oxford, previously an Anglican priest.

It is phenomenal that a group of this caliber, representing some of the best training available at the time, should be drawn to a Christian community of less than one hundred thousand souls. It is also remarkable how well their work stands up under current scholarship (which will be substantiated by some examples from that literature). It is significant, too, how well their thought applies to our own era (with some reinterpretation necessary, most notably as it applies to the concept of Testimony).

The original intention of this work was to provide a guide and supplement to Robert Barclay's *Apology* (1676 Latin, 1678 English), which was analyzed to lift out the doctrines that were its implied presuppositions. In comparing Barclay's work with that of the others named above, it soon became apparent that although their starting points were sometimes different, or the way in which they developed a particular area of doctrine varied, there was considerable substantive agreement among them. Not only did they supplement one another, but they all looked to George Fox for their basic orientation and structure.

Since the *Apology* furnishes a more orderly and sustained treatment of most topics than the other authors' writings, it provides the major portion of the quotations used here. There are liberal quotations from George Fox and the others, and the extent to which they parallel or supplement one another is pointed out where it is of special significance.

Rather than impede the start of the treatment of thought of these writers, further consideration of method and my own presuppositions has been deferred to the Appendices. Finally, a personal comment. This work is the culmination of a long pilgrimage in the recovery and broadening of a faith that was severely damaged by World War II. I was first attracted to Friends by their neighborly acts in Seattle in reintegrating the nisei into the daily life and business activities of the Pacific Northwest. I became an adherent when some of the faith in Christ that motivated others at Shrewsbury, New Jersey, reaffirmed my conviction that such persons were Christians in fact as well as in theory. For over a decade, I have been basking in Manasquan meeting's concerned Christianity.

Work on Barclay over a period of twenty years and more recently on Fox and the others convinced me that a route to deeper acquaintance with their thought and inspiration ought to be provided for those lacking the time or the patience to approach their works directly.

—*Dean Freiday*

Chapter 1
THE GOSPEL

The "epistle" to Charles II in the *Apology* makes it clear that Barclay has no intention of using his essay as a vehicle for flattery, "the usual design of such works." Nor is it written to obtain the king's patronage. It is a prophetic call for the king's personal reformation. It reminds him of the great things that God has done for him and urges him to "turn to the Lord" with all his heart, to rule justly, and to defend religious liberty.

The opening salutation in the epistle also states Barclay's own mission, that of "a servant of Jesus Christ, called of God to the Dispensation of the Gospel . . . commanded to be preached to all nations." Similarly, the Introduction reiterates that he is among several "whom God has chosen to be dispensers of this Gospel," [3] which was described to the king as the "Gospel of Christ . . . the Power of God unto salvation," and which was being revealed again "after a long dark night of apostasy."

Later quotations [110, 123] reveal that Barclay's primary text is Revelation 14:6-7 KJB: "And I saw another angel fly in the midst of heaven, having the everlasting gospel to preach . . . to every nation, and kindred, and tongue, and people, saying . . . the hour of his judgment is come . . . ." Both Fox and Barclay distinguish this "everlasting Gospel" from what has frequently been referred to in modern contemporary terms as "privatistic salvation."

The statements of two bishops who were contemporaries of Barclay are pertinent. Edward Stillingfleet preached a sermon on "the advantages of Christianity as the way to happiness." John Wilkins stated that "the great end of religion" is "to make men happy."[1] For centuries popular preaching has been "inclined to put the emphasis above all, if not even exclusively, on the joys of the reward and the pains of punishment" as Jacques Maritain has characterized its form today.[2] Leslie Dewart suspects that preaching "salvation" in terms of "going to heaven" and "avoiding hell" fairly faithfully reflects not only Medieval Scholastic theology, but the Church's teaching from quite early in its history.

Dewart labels this salvific search for happiness (or "beatitude") a "spiritual hedonism." He sees it as a vast oversimplification that justified Freud's characterization of popular religion as an illusion, one that on one hand explained the riddle of the Christian's world "with an enviable completeness" and on the other saw the Christian as under a "solicitous Providence" that would make up "for any shortcomings in this life . . . in a future existence."[3]

The Gospel being reproclaimed by Fox and Barclay begins in very personal terms, as any teaching about redemption must. However, it has broader implications, not only for personal life and hope, but in terms of wider responsibilities as well, and without denying a future judgment it emphasizes current judgment. This Gospel, Barclay states, "is the universal evangelical principle" [123] so near to you that it is "on your lips . . . in your heart." The Scripture alluded to is Romans 10:8, which actually refers to "the Word," but this and other quotations indicate that for Barclay the Word and the Gospel are "one and the same." [104]

"The tiny thing which reproves" people "in their hearts is nothing less than the Gospel preached in them." By it "Christ is trying to save their souls." [122] Even where the "outward preaching . . . is unknown" [7] "there is still "honor, glory, and peace" for "everyone who does good." [116] Indeed the possibility of this "universal redemption . . . makes Christ's Preaching truly the Gospel, or the annunciation of the Glad Tidings" for all mankind. [78-79]

This is not "another Gospel" (Gal. 1:6 TEV), or a "new Gospel," but new insights into the same Gospel preached by Christ and His disciples. [63-65] Because it is not a new Gospel, no new miracles are required as confirmation. [189] What is required is to believe this Gospel *and* accept its implications. "Salvation does not lie in the literal knowledge of the name 'Jesus,' but in the experience of what it signifies . . . . If those who have never heard of Adam are injured by his Fall . . . why can't they be saved by the gift and grace of Christ?" Salvation is by the experience of His Power, *[113]* and "those who were aware of their inclination toward sin and also of the inward Power and salvation which come from Christ were saved, whether . . . before or after his appearance in the flesh." *[116]* "As the apostle said, 1 Corinthians 10:4-5 [RSV], all ate the same supernatural food and all drank the same supernatural drink. For they drank from the supernatural Rock which followed them, and the Rock was Christ.'" *[28, 330]*

Light/Grace, and conversion are difficult things to comprehend with the mind. *[87]* The brain "is not the proper organ" by which to know God. Although it cannot be denied "that man can apprehend and know spiritual things with his brain," purely mental knowledge in such matters "hinders him" rather than advancing "him toward salvation." *[91]*

To answer those whose Platonist background caused them to see the Light proclaimed by the Quakers as a "natural light," Barclay temporarily adopts philosophical language rather than his usual biblical terminology. He spells out the roles of "reason" and "inspiration," so typical of his opponents' theologies, by stating: God "has given man the Light of his Son . . . to rule him in things spiritual and the light of reason to rule him in things natural." Nevertheless, even man's reason can be "enlightened by this divine and pure Light" and "such enlightened reason may also be useful to men even in spiritual things if it is kept subservient to the Spirit and the true Light is followed and obeyed." *[91]*

Belief alone will not inform us of the will of God for us. "Inward manifestation in the heart" is necessary. *[103-104]* "The Psalmist calls not for speculation, but sensation: 'Taste and see that the Lord is good' (Psalm 30:8)." The best and truest knowledge of God is not that wrought by the "sweat of the brain, but that which is kindled within us, by a heavenly warmth in our hearts" (quoted from John Smith, the Cambridge Platonist). *[21]* This is what Scripture means when it states that having had a "taste of the heavenly gift and a share in the Holy Spirit, when they have experienced the goodness of God's Word and the spiritual energies of the age to come." (Heb. 6:4-5 NEB) *[166]* "We learn through living experience how to overcome evil and its temptations by following the Lord, walking in his Light, and waiting daily for the direct revelation of Wisdom and Knowledge." *[197]*

Others have experienced this too, particularly the Catholic mystics who "have known and tasted the Love of God, and have felt the Power and Virtue of God's Spirit working with them for their salvation." *[247]* Even "some of the pagan philosophers knew the remedy for evil, but did not know His name." *[118]* This is the "Light to all nations" that the Prophet Isaiah speaks of in Isaiah 49:6. *[113]* It is "the Light spoken of in John" (1:45), who "is Christ," *[330]* the "true Light that gives light to every man." (John 1:9 NIV)

This is "Christ in you, the hope of glory." (Col. 1:27 RSV) *[146]* "Become a fool for Christ's sake, in order to know his teaching in your heart." Learn from him "who makes all things manifest . . . and who reproves . . . by his Light. (Eph. 5:13)" In the words of Titus 2:11-14 (TEV), which Barclay chose for the title page of the *Apology:* "God has revealed his grace for the salvation of all mankind. That grace instructs us to give up ungodly living and worldly passions, and to live self-controlled, upright, and godly lives in this world, as we wait for the blessed Day we hope for, when the glory of our great God and Savior Jesus Christ will appear. He gave himself for us, to rescue us from all wickedness and to make us a pure people who belong to him alone and are eager to do good."

The Titus quotation could almost be a summary of what Quakers emphasized in proclaiming the Gospel afresh. It opens on the note that grace has been revealed and that it is ready to instruct us how to live "self-controlled, upright, and godly lives." There is an apocalyptic framework. The last times – the times of watching and waiting – have been inaugurated. "Our great God and Savior Jesus Christ" who sacrificed Himself to rescue us stands ready "to make us a pure people" of undivided loyalty, eager and committed to doing good. These are all themes that will recur again and again as Barclay's theology unfolds.

The Risen One Judges and Instructs

Nowhere in the *Apology* is there an explicit statement of Fox's central dictum: "Christ has come to teach his people himself," but all the elements of Fox's affirmation are present. The Titus quotation emphasizes that "grace instructs." Elsewhere Barclay states: "We know that he has risen and has been revealed in Spirit." This is not limited to the experience recorded in the New Testament, but is still applicable. Christ is the risen Lord who is present to His faithful followers now. "He is leading his children . . . that they may walk with him in his Light." *[361]*

Christ's leading is not limited to instruction in matters of faith and belief. He also judges our unrighteousness and leads into holiness and purity. "The principal reason for Christ's appearance was the *removal* [italics added] of sin and the gathering of a righteous generation that would serve the Lord in purity of mind," *[158]* a people who are "wholly devoted to doing God's will." (Col. 4:12 NEB) For under grace "sin shall no longer be your master . . . you are no longer under law, but under the grace of God." *[162]*

Indeed God has granted those willing to "turn to him" the possibility of such stability that "total and final apostasy [will be] impossible." He has already "given many of his people the assurance that they are his and that no power can pluck them from his hand. He is ready to give all of them this complete and positive assurance" in order that they may be "confirmed beyond all doubt and hesitation." *[168-170]*

But if this is to happen, we must first *cease* doing evil before we can learn to do good (Isa. 1:16-17 – emphasis added). *[279]*

Gospel is a theme second only to Christ in importance for Barclay. Not only does the word "Gospel" occur at least 84 times in the *Apology*, but, in virtually interchangeable words, the time/state/dispensation/age/era of the Gospel is said to be here. There is a fresh pouring out of the Spirit, a plenitude of grace, a New Covenant. Much that was important under the Old Covenant ended with Christ, who was and is the Substance, and the fulfillment of the legal practices, rites, ceremonies, types, and figures under the Law. This is the "Time when God proposed . . . to restore again the ancient simplicity of Truth." It is a time of beginning again, not simply reforming or altering divergent practices.

This is a neo-apostolic era: "In our day God has reared many witnesses for himself, just as he gathered the fishermen of old." *[205]* "In our age . . . God has raised faithful witnesses and evangelists . . . to preach again his everlasting Gospel." *[123]* "A very faithful testimony has been given by the witnesses whom God has raised in this age. It is beyond anything that has been generally known or practiced for many generations." *[384]* "In this age . . . there are many" whom God "has inwardly redeemed . . . from the world" so completely that it "used to be considered possible only for those who were cloistered or in monasteries." *[394]*

By way of definition, Barclay declares: "Whoever preaches the Gospel is an evangelist." *[213]* "God has raised us up to preach Christ, and to direct people to his pure Light in their hearts . . . . Through the operation of the cross of Christ . . . we have denied our own wisdom and forfeited our own will." *[111]* "He has sent us forth to preach the everlasting Gospel to all." Its message is that "Christ is near to all." He is "the Light in all, the

Seed sown in the hearts of all." We rejoice that we have been required to lay aside our own wisdom and learning "in order to learn of [i.e., "from"] Jesus. Let us sit down at the feet of Jesus in our hearts and hear him who makes all things manifest" and reproves "by his Light." (Eph. 5:13) *[110]*

The "everlasting Gospel," spelled out in a little greater detail is that

> In his obedience to the will of the Father and by the eternal Spirit, Jesus Christ offered up his earthly body as a propitiation for the remission of sins. He finished his testimony on earth with a most perfect example of patience, resignation, and holiness so that all might partake of the fruit of that sacrifice.
>
> He also poured forth into the hearts of all men a measure of the divine Light and Seed with which he is clothed. In that way he reaches into the consciences of all men in order to raise them up out of death and darkness by his Life and Light. In that way they may partake of his Body and have fellowship with the Father and with the Son. *[331]*

Notes to Chapter 1

Italic figures in brackets within the text refer to page numbers in *Barclay's Apology in Modern English*, edited and published by Dean Freiday.

1 The Stillingfleet sermon title is given in John Wilkins's *Ecclesiastes: Or a Discourse Concerning the Gift of Preaching as It Falls Under the Rules of Art*, 8th Edition (London: J. Lawrence, 1704), p. 145. Wilkins's own wording is from p. 140 of that volume, first published in 1646.

2 Quoted by Leslie Dewart, *The Future of Belief: Theism in a World Come of Age* (New York: Herder and Herder, 1966), p. 28 from Jacques Maritain, *Moral Philosophy* (London: 1964), p. 79.

3 Dewart, *op.cit.*, pp. 22-35. The Freud quotation, found on p. 22, is from Freud's *Civilization and its Discontents* (London, 1930), p. 23.

Chapter 2

RIGHTEOUSNESS, HOLINESS, AND REGENERATION

The everlasting Gospel is neither a sop to assuage guilty consciences nor a false declaration that men are "just" who continue to be unjust. It is a remedy for evil that calls for "inward change and renewal . . . true penitence," *[127]* and "conformity to Christ." *[131]* Indeed, "the main purpose of Christianity" is to "renew and reform the hearts of the individuals within the church." *[178]* "Those who do not follow Christ's commands and who are not clothed with his righteousness and compassion are not his disciples." *[183-184]* Then Barclay adds a personal note: "While I was still only 18 years old," God "made me seriously consider (as I hope he will others) the fact that no man can see God without holiness and regeneration." *[206]* "A Christian without grace is no Christian at all." *[193]*

"The most important thing for a Christian is to crucify the natural inclinations of the human will in order to allow God to govern both his actions and his desires." *[265]* For "daily tasks are done in another Spirit . . . when the mind is leavened by the love of God." *[410]* Unlike Calvinists, Quakers cannot "live comfortably with their sins." *[109]* The reference is to "the words of the Westminster Larger Catechism: 'it is impossible for a man, even the best of men, to be free of sin in this life.'" *[155]* But, "none should deceive themselves and think that they are justified by the death and sufferings of Christ as long as sin lies at their door (Gen. 4:7 KJV), iniquity prevails, and they are still unrenewed and unregenerate." *[147]* This can also be stated in other ways. "As it is most often used in Scripture, justification refers to making one just, rather than merely having the reputation for being just. It is the equivalent of sanctification." *[135]* And "it is expressly stated in 2 Cor. 6:14 that there is no communion between light and darkness." *[157]*

The key question is: "To what extent can Christ prevail in us while we are alive?" *[155]* The answer to this is really a matter of extremes. It is equally erroneous to maintain that it is impossible to fall from grace in the slightest degree, as it "is to deny the possibility of achieving sufficient increase and stability in the truth to make total and final apostasy impossible." *[168]* Nevertheless, "to those who patiently persist in doing the best of which they are capable; and who seek glory, honor, and immortality in that way; life eternal is offered." *[138]* Lest they shall be under any delusion that justification is their own work, they need to be reminded that it is "based on the power, virtue, and grace of Christ," which renew the heart. *[126]* For it is by grace that we become clothed with Him, "and our souls live according to God's own pure and holy image of righteousness." *[147]*

Perfection and Stability

"Perfection is attributed only to the reborn man who has been raised by Christ and renewed in his mind . . . He will be led by the Spirit, which not only reproves sin, but provides the power to overcome it." *[156]* "Perfection is the purpose for which we receive the Gospel," *[162]* but "not a perfection that has no room for daily growth." And it is not a perfection which does not require "attention to that of God" in the heart if one is not to "fall into iniquity and lose it." *[156]*

"Nevertheless a state can be attained in this life in which it becomes so natural to act righteously that a condition of stability is achieved in which sin is impossible . . . One of the Apostles has clearly asserted [this] . . . in 1 John 3:9 NEB: 'A child of God does not commit sin, because the divine seed remains in him; he cannot be a sinner, because he is God's child.'" *[157]* If this seems too high a claim, another Apostle has stated: "God's people are said, even while here, to 'come to share in the very being of God' (2 Pet. 1:4 NEB)," and to be "one with Christ, spiritually (1 Cor. 6:17)." *[157]*

"Certainly if Christ's coming served its purpose, the members of his Church are not always sinning in thought, word, and deed. There would be no difference then between being sanctified and unsanctified, clean and unclean, holy and unholy." *[159]* After all, the goal is "mature manhood, measured by nothing less than the full stature of Christ." (Eph. 4:11-13 NEB) *[160]*

Salvation Is Not a Once-and-for-All-Time Experience

Salvation or reconciliation is not a single experience. The conditions governing it "must be met throughout life." *[136]* Christ's sacrificial death was "the opening of the door to God's mercy," which became "effective for everyone who is willing to receive his inward appearance," *[139]* and which by being accepted brings about their conversion. *[226]* A beginning is being made when you "turn your mind to the Light of Christ and his Spiritual law in your heart and allow its reproofs," *[163]* then "Christ continues to make intercession so that everyone may . . . continue and go on and not . . . faint or go back again." *[138-139]*

"A spiritual, celestial, and invisible principle, a principle in which God dwells as Father, Son, and Spirit . . . exists as a seed in all men which . . . draws, invites, and inclines the individual toward God. Some call this the *vehiculum Dei,* or the spiritual body of Christ, the flesh and blood of Christ which came down from heaven, and on which all who have faith are fed and nourished with eternal life." *[85]* "Although we affirm that Christ dwells in us, it is not without a mediator . . . whereas in Jesus himself there was no mediator. He was the Eternal Word, which was with God and was God. He is as the Head and we are the members. He is the vine and we are the branches." *[86]*

"God does not delight in evil, but abhors transgression," nevertheless He pities the transgressor and "provides a way out of his misdeeds." *[157]* It is Christ's Light which exercises judgment "upon the unrighteous part in you" if you will allow it "to become victorious." *[163]* For the Light of Christ in your conscience is "like a sharp two-edged sword . . . . Like fire and a hammer" it will forge away all that belonged to the natural man. *[105]* "God, in and by" the Light and Seed of His own Son, "invites, calls, exhorts, and strives with every man in order to save him." *[82]* He grants "sufficient grace for salvation." *[94, 99]* "Everyone receives enough . . . and requires no more." *[102]*

"Let no one be so bold as to mock God and assume that he is justified and accepted in the sight of God by virtue of Christ's death and sufferings if he remains unjustified in his own heart. His hope will prove to be that of the hypocrite and he will perish." *[154]* "Turn toward righteousness" *[174]* and be "engrafted in Christ." *[175]*

Then as often as you "turn to him with genuine repentance," you will "partake of the fulness of his merits," and have "true ground for the hope and belief" that you are justified. *[147]* "Run straight toward the goal in order to win the prize, which is God's call through Christ Jesus to the life above." (Phil. 3:14 TEV) *[165]*

"This doctrine . . . exalts above everything else the grace of God . . . . Not only the first motions and beginnings of good are ascribed to God's grace, but also the whole conversion and salvation of the soul." *[83]* "There is nothing required . . . that is not taught by God's grace." *[112]* "For those who do not resist the Light, but receive it, it becomes a holy, pure and spiritual birth in them. It produces holiness, righteousness, purity." By it "Jesus Christ is formed" in them, and they are "sanctified and justified." *[125]*

As we walk with Him we "share together a common life." (1 John 1:7 NEB) *[100]* "The Gospel is not merely a declaration of good things, 'it is the saving power of God for everyone who has faith.' (Rom. 1:16 NEB) . . . It reveals to the soul what is good, just, and righteous. As the soul accepts this and believes, the degree of righteousness becomes greater and faith advances from one stage to another." *[103]*

"Embrace the Son while the Day lasts!" *[112]*

Italic figures in brackets within the text refer to page numbers in *Barclay's Apology in Modern English.*

Chapter 3

AUTHENTICITY, GENUINENESS, TRUTH

Truth is another topic like Gospel and Righteousness that runs throughout the entire *Apology* but is never treated under a specific heading. Far from being turned into a mere Shibboleth or slogan by endless repetitive usage, Truth is instead a note that is emphasized by being brought out in a thousand different ways. Just as one tests good crystal stemware by thumping it to hear its ring, every statement, every belief, every practice is tested against the touchstone of Truth. Anything that smacks of untruth is labeled hypocrisy, or if of a blatant form it is called a lie. But anything that rings true is evaluated by the scriptural terms "equity" or "integrity."

The note of Truth becomes like a melody that keeps repeating endlessly in your brain. Or it is like the loving heckling of an indulgent mother. The *Apology* keeps repeating over and over again this emphasis on Truth as a call to genuineness and authenticity. "True" and "truly" modify thirty different words that describe the Christian faith in all its personal, structural, doctrinal, and practical aspects.

The "true Church" [175, 187] receives a "true Call" [181, 183] and is "truly gathered" [173] to "true faith" [16] and "true Knowledge" [17] by the "true Light." [91] The outcome is a "true religion," [177] a "true Christianity," [298] with "true marks" of faith. [54] "True evangelists" [213] "truly propagate" [367] the "true learning" [197] and cultivate "true ground" [147] and "true tenderness of spirit," [361] and often through "true Christian suffering," [384] they have attained the "true substance," [191] expressed through a "truly spiritual" worship [243] and "true righteousness and holiness," *[252]* which are of the "very nature of grace." *[196]* These "true prophets" (Ep. to Chas. II) are "true ministers" *[193, 198, 213, 224, 231]* who practice "true prayer" *[289]* and "true preaching." *[282]* "True communion" *[344]* is realized through a "true Supper," *[333]* and all things are done in a "true Christian spirit."

The first impression is almost one of obsession with Truth. And since the claim of "Truth" is made in each particular case for a Quaker doctrine or practice, one wonders if some holier-than-thouness might be involved. Deeper analysis, however, reveals that the connecting thread is not that of pride, but an attempt to witness with authenticity and integrity and to avoid a separation between the theoretical and the actual in every understanding of existence and responsibility.

Turning to the scriptural bases, Fr. McKenzie points out[1] that Hebrew "has no distinct word for true and truth." Such ideas are expressed by *'emet*, which means "firmness or solidity." It is applied in particular to "words or personal conduct." Hence such statements or acts can be seen in terms of "'truth' or 'truthfulness' or 'fidelity.'" Furthermore, the "basis on which belief rests" is the "solidity," or "perhaps better," the "reality of its object."

Several further dimensions of the Old Testament idea of Truth are developed by another Catholic reference work.[2] One is "faithfulness," which is regarded as a major aspect of man's response to God's Truth. "Men of truth" (Exod. 18:21; Neh. 7:2) are "men of trust," and "ordinarily *truth* used of men applies directly to their *faithfulness to the covenant* and to divine law," or in other words, applies to "the entire moral posture of the just." Truth has a revelatory aspect elsewhere in the Old Testament, and in that usage it "becomes synonymous with Wisdom."

This lack of a distinct term for "true" and "truth" in the Hebrew vocabulary makes the Greek usage in the New Testament somewhat different, although in at least one passage, 1 Peter 5:12, there is a near parallel to its Old Testament connotation of solidity and steadfastness. In that case the reference is to the Grace of God. Not infrequently "truth" is used "in opposition to unrighteousness," and it "seems to be synonymous with righteousness as an attribute of character or conduct . . . the real or the genuine as opposed to the unreal or the spurious."

Rudolf Bultmann[3] "pointed out that truth in John has a peculiar and distinctively Christian force." There "Truth" is predicated "in a rather peculiar sense, always of Jesus: the true Light (Jn. 1:9), the true Vine (Jn. 15:1). His body is true food and his blood is true drink (Jn. 6:55). In the same sense, the heavenly tabernacle is the true tabernacle (Heb. 8:2)." True here acquires the sense of "permanent and lasting . . . rooted in its heavenly and incorruptible character."

"Jesus Himself is the Way, the Truth, and the Life (Jn. 14:6) . . . full of Grace and Truth (Jn. 1:14)." Thus (for Bultmann) "Truth is the divinely revealed reality of God, manifested in the words and the person of Jesus Christ . . . the ultimate and the supreme Truth." This is also characteristic, with some exceptions, of the Pauline writings. Not only is Truth there "usually the revelation of God through and in Jesus Christ," but "there is no other truth than this."

In addition to the scriptural background, to understand the thrust of Barclay's repeated use, one should keep the seventeenth century context in mind, for there is a basic premise behind all of these affirmations. The point is that Friends were convinced that neither the Continental nor English Reformations had gone far enough in attempting to restore the Church to its primitive purity. They saw centuries of accumulated distortions in theology and departures from apostolic practice that they regarded as apostate. The scandalous moral deviations were so flagrant at the time of the Reformation that any claim that the Church remained unspotted or undefiled could only be regarded as hypocritical. In nearly every aspect of its being the Church had gone astray.

Let us look again at the series of statements above, quoted from the *Apology* in which "true" or similar modifiers figured, with this background in mind. The concept of "Church" had gotten so far removed from its New Testament basis that in everyday conversation the word *church* suggested a "steeple house," or the building in which the Church met rather than the congregation. In other words a metonymical meaning had replaced the substantive one. For those who thought in specifically theological ways, there had been another important shift. The institutional Church had replaced the spiritual Body.

An unbroken physical succession replaced any claim to a succession of holiness and faithfulness, and the moral imperatives originally intrinsic to all doctrine had been crippled. Theologians had found verbal formulations that permitted the Church to sidestep most demands for holiness, discipleship, and service. Christ was not – they claimed – either a model for imitation or a measure of perfection. That quality of life – they said – was confined uniquely to the early Church.

Since the third century, Christians had been divided into "clergy" and "laity." Erecting this distinction upon the flimsiest exegesis of a single New Testament passage (1 Pet. 5:3), ministry thereby tended to become the monopoly of the clergy. There was no longer attention to the divine "Call," and their calling was shifted from God's shoulders to those of institutional administrators. There was no such thing as a divinely "Gathered" Church. The Congregationalists interpreted "gathering" as voluntary association to form a congregation. Tyndale had uniformly translated *ekklesia* "congregation," (in which he had the backing of St. Jerome's Vulgate), but the King James Version replaced congregation with "church." Actually, the word *church* had originally derived from *kyriakon,* meaning "the Lord's." But the transferred derivation broke the association with the living Lord, making it increasingly easy to undergird institutional rather than spiritual ideas wherever it was theologically or administratively advantageous to do so.

It is true that loud claims for "true faith" and "true knowledge" were made in the established church, but the derivation of these claims was positivistic – that is, based upon the declarations and official pronouncements of the institutional church, whose authority was deemed superior to that of any New Testament evidence. While Protestants shifted the locus of authority[4] – in some cases making it collegial or presbyteral, in others making it biblical to the point of biblicism (as Luther did to some degree, and the Puritans did to a greater extent) – nevertheless claims to authenticity usually tended to be stated in at least philosophical if not specifically Scholastic terms. God had been given an Aristotelian or Platonic education so that he issued ultimata in Hellenistic relativisms rather than in prophetic absolutes.

The "true marks" for a faith that seemed to be neither true religion nor true Christianity had become difficult to discern. Where was the "one, holy, catholic, and apostolic" Church? By any empirical tests its division was obvious, its immorality scandalous, and its claimed universality was in point of fact exclusiveness and narrowness. It was very difficult to find any aspect of its structure or practice, and very few aspects of its doctrine, that could be labeled truly "apostolic." And to gain acceptance as such for some points, credibility had to be stretched to the utmost in order to make the mutations seem legitimate.

In the face of all this there arose "the first publishers of Truth," a new crop of evangelists. They claimed to be called to proclaim *again* the authentic and "everlasting Gospel" as it had been proclaimed in the apostles' days. The content of their proclamation was that of the teaching, ground, and principles by which the first and truest Christians had been "truly redeemed." Their mission was to "truly propagate" this Gospel afresh and to all mankind.

Those gathered to Christ by the Spirit's call through these "true evangelists" received a "true baptism" of the Spirit-and-fire, which washed away or cauterized all unrighteousness and uncleanness. They were bereft of their own wills and were "truly spiritual" in their freely given obedience to their risen Lord. Their "true repentance" and "true tenderness of Spirit" had often been achieved only through "true christian suffering" — whether by distraint of material goods, imprisonment, or deprivation of civil rights. The real substance of the Christian faith had been revealed when all comfort and support but that of the immovable One Himself had been taken away. Christ Jesus alone could speak to their condition, and in His compassion He lent His presence and solace wherever they were forced to go, or in whatever they had to endure.

A "truly spiritual" worship under His direct guidance revealed His will for them. Nothing extraneous to this purpose was admitted. The quality of their lives was their testimony and witness to the holiness of Him whom they worshiped. They realized that righteousness, equity, and integrity were not only of the "very nature of grace," [196] but of the essence of the Church. "Unspottedness" could not be claimed where, in fact, it did not exist. Unless there was transparent righteousness, the Church ceased to exist where it had gone astray.

These "true prophets" flattered no one and knew subservience only to God. "True preaching" was not solely didactical or hortatory but included the intuitions that had grown out of shared experience and had been developed by faithful witness and service. "True prayer" was a renewed emptying of self and an opening up to Grace and Light.

"True communion" was not reducible to a symbolic rite, but demanded a "true Supper" where the sustenance was spiritual. The branches were fed by the life-giving Grace and Power of the Vine. Every act, in individual daily commerce as well as in the "Gathered" community, had to be an act of praise to the Creator and a fit use of His creation. Everything was done in a "true Christian spirit." And although it does not seem to have been made explicit in previous Quaker theological studies, there was also an implied Testimony for Consistency. Just as God was declared not to be whimsical or changeable but consistent in His dealings with His people, they in their turn were to be consistent in their behavior.

Life was not to be divided into separate compartments with different standards. Murder was murder in war as well as in peace; unequivocal speech was to be used in daily conversation as well as in a court of law. Other examples will be given when we look at the implications of faith for practice in greater detail.

Notes to Chapter 3

Italic figures in brackets within the text refer to page numbers in *Barclay's Apology in Modern English.*

1 John L. McKenzie, S.J., *Dictionary of the Bible* (Milwaukee: Bruce, 1965), s.v. "truth" and "faith."
2 Ignace de la Potterie, S.J., "truth," in *Dictionary of Biblical Theology,* ed. by Xavier Leon-Dufour, S.J. (New York: Desclee, 1967), pp. 545-548.
3 McKenzie states, *loc. cit.*
4 Cf. my *The Bible—its Criticism, Interpretation and Use—in 16th- and 17th-Century England* (Catholic and Quaker Studies No. 4, 1979) and also my "The Early Quakers and the Doctrine of Authority," *Quaker Religious Thought,* vol. 15, no. 1(Aut. '73):4-38.

Chapter 4

THE CHURCH AND MINISTRY

Previously matters of faith that pertain primarily "to the individual have been dealt with." Now the things will be considered which "relate to the joint fellowship and communion of Christians as they come under an outward and visible society . . . called the Church of God and compared to a body in the Scriptures . . . the Body of Christ . . . . Members in this spiritual and Mystical Body possess different gifts of Grace and of the Spirit. From this diversity arises the distinction between individuals in the visible society of Christians, whereby some are apostles, some pastors, evangelists, ministers, and so forth." *[171-172]*

The paragraph just quoted from Barclay approaches both the Church and the ministry in terms that would not be used by Fox. There are significant differences between them in the ways in which they spell out the nature of the Church, although both tend to emphasize that joint "fellowship" and "communion" are of the very essence of the Church. Both of these English words stem from *koinonia* and they derive from its root meaning, which is to share either spiritual or material things. Those who participate in such sharing constitute a union or communion as far as spiritual matters are concerned.

"It is a fellowship that has no parallels. Its unique character comes from its unique Lord."[1] This *koinonia*, or the community that shares and communicates together, is of such vital significance for any dynamic understanding of "Church," that Yves Congar states: "In her ultimate reality the Church is men's fellowship with God and with one another in Christ."[2] Thus it is primarily the interaction between individuals who have been

"Gathered" by God into the Presence of Christ and their Communication/Communion with Him and with each other that constitutes the Church.

In the New Testament "gathering" is the common denominator for both the aggregation of persons and the process that produces this community although various words are used to describe it—"church, community, congregation, assembly," even "synagogue." The latter term, however, in most books of the New Testament is confined largely to specifically Jewish assemblies. The exception is the book of Revelation.

According to a Roman Catholic biblical theologian[3] it was apparently "some time before the early Christians realized their union in Christ in terms of *ekklesia*." In secular Greek the word *ekklesia* referred to the assembly composed primarily of citizens in a self-governing Greek city-state; and Acts 19:39 applies it in that way to Ephesus. In the Septuagint, however, *ekklesia* was used to translate *qahal*, the "assembly" or "congregation" of the Israelites.

Modern European languages divide into two groups according to the etymological roots of the words they use for "Church." The Romanic or Celtic languages use *Eglise, Iglesia, Chiesa,* or *Eglwys,* for example. These are derived from *ekklesia*. The other group borrows from *kyriakon* (literally, "[thing] of the Lord" or "belonging to the Lord"). They use *Kirche, Kirk,* or *Church*. The latter word seems to come into English (according to the *O.E.D.*) by way of pre-Christian usage. The Germans applied it to the places where Christians met, although the priority of place or building—rather than congregation—is far from an open-and-shut case.

While the first use in English (in the seventh century) was a legal reference to a church building, and it seems to have been a century or two before the word was applied to the *household* of God instead of the Lord's *house*, this may be due only to the fact that legal records are better preserved than more casual references. And legal references would be more likely to deal with tangible property rights. In the New Testament, on the other hand, while *Kyriakos* is used as the adjective in Lord's Day, Lord's Supper, and other cultic or theological terms, it is never applied to the place where Christians met.

In its denominational name the Assembly of God picks up one aspect of the New Testament emphases on the congregation rather than the edifice. Similarly Jehovah's Witnesses use "Kingdom hall" for their gathering place. In so doing these churches remind us that the first buildings constructed specifically for church purposes (when for one reason or another Christians no longer met in homes) were called *basilicas* (a name now reserved for specially designated large church buildings). The root word here was *Basileia*, the Kingdom of God.

Theologically speaking, the majority of the linguistic and exegetical evidence is on the side of "congregation, gathering, assembly, or community." And *The Modern Concordance to the New Testament*, edited by Michael Darton, which is based on related ideas rather than individual words or phrases, sees the generic concept as "gathering." It is a primary or closely secondary meaning for five of the eleven terms that are grouped under that word.

This etymological background will be useful as we examine both Barclay's and Fox's approaches to ecclesiology.

There is an early borrowing of categories from non-Quaker sources in Barclay's discussion in the opening paragraph of the present chapter.[4] Barclay has already mentioned "visible societies," and later he will refer to both visible and invisible churches.[5] Fox tends to avoid this categorization.

Lewis Benson has stated that for Fox the *reality* of the Church is "a dynamic relationship to a living being." This relationship was brought about by answering Christ's call to discipleship. It is His *calling* and *gathering* that created a faithful and obedient people. Once those who dwelt in darkness "were not a people, but are now the people of God." (1 Pet. 2:10 KJV) They are "God's own people, chosen to proclaim the wonderful acts of God." (1 Pet. 2:9 TEV) They are a New Covenant community that exists "only where the master-disciple relationship to the living Christ is experienced."[6]

This dynamic personal relationship "between God's people and God's Son" is the one and only "root and ground that can serve as the basis for church government and order."[7] It "involves not only hearing the Master but obeying him." It is by no means "a voluntary association of religionists" who set their own goals and objectives.[8]

"Faith is the ground of this community when faith is understood to mean putting one's whole existence under the Authority of Christ . . . . The life of this community is not sustained and upheld by perpetual ordinances and rules of succession. It is not a community that is started just once, in one place, and then expands from this one point. It is a community that comes into existence where faith exists and which withers and fades where faith languishes . . . . When faith ends this community ends. But Christ can create this community out of nothing through faith."9

While for Fox the "inner life" of the Church "has the character of a spiritual organism and not that of a human institution,"10 "based on rational or practical principles" the Church is "a community with historical existence" so long as it remains faithful and obedient. "It has social cohesion and functions as a social organism and not as a mere collective,"11 but its very existence depends upon faithfulness to Christ's own *gathering* and *ordering*. Christ Himself authenticates its testimony and witness "by honouring you with his blessed Presence."12

The local "gatherings" or "assemblies" in Christ's name are almost invariably referred to as Churches of Christ by Fox and the other authors cited in this work. "Every believer in the Light (which is the Life in Christ)," Fox says, "is a member of Christ's Church and grafted into him. And so he is the holy Head of the Church and they are heirs of his Order."

Fox also refers to Hebrews 12:22, 23, which speaks of the "joyful gathering of God's first-born sons . . . good people made perfect" (TEV), a passage that harks back to the New Creation in Isaiah 65:18, 19. The Church that is in God the Father of Christ must be washed, sanctified, and cleansed (1 Cor. 6:11). "The true Christian fellowship is with the Father, and with the Son" [1 Jn. 1:3], by whom all things were made and created [Col. 1:16, Eph. 3:9], and all fellowships below that will come to nothing.13 "We are Christians and partake of the Nature [2 Pet. 1:4] and Life [2 Cor. 4:10] of Christ."14 As "children of the everlasting Kingdom" (2 Pet. 1:11), we "serve and worship God in righteousness and holiness" (Heb. 12:28),15 "in Spirit and in Truth." (Jn. 4:23-24)16

"The true Church [is] known again." Its members are "not of the world, but are gathered and gathering out of it." "The Lord is gathering his people by his Spirit and Light and Grace and Truth."17 They who are "made alive by Christ, are a living Church." (1 Cor. 15:22) He is gathering them now "from East to West, from North to South." (Mt. 24:31, also perhaps Lk. 13:29) The last days have dawned and "now shall the angel be known that holds the four winds." (Rev. 7:1)18

Most important of all, "where two or three are gathered together in his Name [Mt. 18:20] there is the Church and he is in the midst of them." Be careful therefore to "see that they do not turn away from Christ that speaks from heaven." (Heb. 12:25) "The Church in her glory and beauty is . . . [i.e., "has"] appeared and [is] appearing"19; and it will disappear, and cease to exist if its members do not faithfully follow their Master in righteous-ness and holiness.[20]

While Barclay sometimes comes close to Fox's view of the Church when he uses "visibility" as an adjective to denote an empirical *quality*, by and large Barclay divides the Church into two separate but related units, a rationale that is frequent in much Protestant theology. However, Barclay puts quite different content than these other theologies do into the two terms at certain points. In his understanding of the Church, there are not only *signs* that a spiritual fellowship exists, but there is also a "visible Church," which is the concrete society that admits members and undertakes what are primarily sociological functions.

His companion unit, "the Church invisible," is comprised of all who are "called and truly gathered by God. It includes both those who are still in this inferior world and those who, having already laid down the earthly tabernacle, have passed into their heavenly mansions." Together these present and past Christians make up "the one catholic Church about which there is so much controversy." *[173]*

By declaring "the one catholic Church" and "the Church invisible" to be one and the same, Barclay solves several theological dilemmas at one time. The dogmatic maxim that "outside the Church there can be no salvation" offers no handicap. Since traditionally God alone knows who are members of the Church invisible, Barclay can include in the "invisible Church" those who "have become obedient to the holy Light and Testimony of God in their hearts." Even though they have not had the benefit of either the Scriptures or baptism, if they have "become sanctified" by their obedience to the secret and unknown "Life and Virtue of Jesus" they may join those who are "called from all the corners of the earth" and "sit down with Abraham, Isaac, and Jacob." (Mt. 8:11)

"Men and women of integrity and simplicity of heart" need no preparation to become "members of this catholic Church," whether they are other "sorts of Christians" or "pagans, Turks, and Jews." They have won the universal redemption bought for them and have their names written in heaven. Furthermore, even when the Church does not appear to be empirically visible, it has nevertheless "existed in all generations." There are many who belonged even then, through individual faithfulness. *[173-174]*

The "Church visible also signifies a certain number of persons who have [not only] been gathered by God's Spirit, and by the testimony of some of his servants [but are transformed by the

Grace of Christ]. This visible fellowship has been brought to a belief in the true principles and doctrines of the Christian faith. With their hearts united by the same love, and their understandings informed of the same truths, they gather, meet, and assemble together to wait upon God, to worship him, and to bear a joint testimony for the Truth against error, and to suffer for this Truth." [174]

Anyone committed to a life of righteousness and holiness becomes a member of this "Church catholic" (i.e., the invisible Church), but this is not true for the membership in a "particular church" (i.e., a local congregation). To join a "particular church" not only is the "inward work indispensably necessary, but also profession of belief in Jesus Christ and in the holy truths delivered by his Spirit in the Scriptures." It is absolutely necessary to believe "the outward testimony where God has afforded the opportunity of knowing it." In the "true Church" profession and holiness are both necessary. [175]

In the final analysis, however, "nothing except the gathering of several true Christians into one Body makes a Church. When all the members of a Church lose the Life of Christianity, and it no longer rules in their hearts, the church ceases to exist in that place . . . . They have lost the quality that made them a church . . . [For] when the heavenly inheritance is lost . . . the title returns to Christ." [184-185]

"The Church is defined as the Kingdom of the beloved Son of God into which the people of God are translated . . . . Called the Body of Christ, who is [also] the Head . . . [it is] knit together . . . with a growth that is from God.'" (Col. 2:19) [186] "No man or church, even though it has been truly called by God can retain its power and authority any longer than it retains the Power, the Life, and the righteousness of Christianity." [183]

In these preceding two paragraphs Barclay sounds remarkably like Fox and they are in very close agreement. This is an appropriate point to take up a further elaboration of Fox's understanding of the Church as Arthur Roberts analyzed it in 1954.[21]

The Church of the Restoration

Arthur Roberts set out to discover "a dominant ideal" that would "provide the most suitable framework for the views of George Fox." His investigation showed that it was "his concept of the Church" that proved "to be such an ideal."[22] He also found many "too facile identifications" of Fox's thought with that of his contemporaries. Although Fox "shared much in common with the radical movements of his time . . . efforts to align him neatly with Baptists, Seekers, mystics, Ranters, Fifth-Monarchy, Levellers, and Finders result in only partial and inadequate appraisals." That Fox did not see himself in this way is borne out by his statement that he "maintained the true Church, and the true Head thereof" against the Presbyterians, Baptists, and those who came to be known as Congregationalists, and also the Anglicans in a 1648 dispute with all of them at Leicestershire.[23]

In considering the Church, as in other matters, "Fox is prophetic, not speculative. He is interested in what did happen, what does happen, what will happen in terms of salvation . . . The Scriptures reveal what has happened redemptively up through the coming of Christ. *Present revelation* [italics added] confirms and applies the fulfillment in Christ . . . . It is by the revelation of God that Christ is known in his 'flesh'—his birth, preaching, miracles, sufferings, passion, death, resurrection, and in his divinity. It is the serpent's kingdom which denies present inspiration . . . saying 'there is no such thing to be looked for now-a-days' as God's voice."[24]

To say that "is a veritable denial of the promise Jesus gave of the coming of the Holy Spirit and of this fulfillment amongst the Apostles, and in the succession of 'the true ministers.'"[25] These are defined elsewhere as successors in faithfulness, rather than in any "unbroken chain" sense. "The Church that comes by revelation of God and in the Power of Jesus Christ calls men out of the world by a Restoration of their spiritual natures . . . to restore the Image of God lost in the Fall."[26]

"It is . . . Restoration to communion with God that is the essence of Fox's teaching regarding Perfection. Relationship, not understanding or attainment, is indicated. This is the uniting of persons to Christ as the Head of the Body—the Church . . . 'Christ the heavenly and spiritual man' . . . reforms his believers and followers out of the natural, outward, and carnal into the heavenly, inward, and spiritual."[27] Christ is "priest, mediator, redeemer, Lord, and ruler . . . . The only contact [with God] is in personal, present experience, but it is saved from subjectivism by the unity of inspiration in redemptive history, by the constancy of God, and by the real Presence of Christ in the soul of the believer."

"Restoration to Perfection is the placing of man once more in the Will and Image of God."[28] "Conversion to God was radical to the extent that members of the Church were, in a sense, to all be prophets before the Lord."[29] "Christ as the Life is an extension of the salvation experience to a perfectionism in which the sinful nature is purged by the baptism with the Holy Spirit. Christ, the Head of the Church, is the real Presence in those who are really restored to holiness which is not imputed nor inherent. The mark of the conversion experience is Victory."[30]

This victorious and genuine faithfulness led Fox to define the Church as "the pillar and ground of Truth" in the light of 1 Timothy 3:15. The *Jerusalem Bible* translates this vividly: "I wanted you to know how people ought to behave in God's family – that is, in the Church of the living God, which upholds the truth and keeps it safe." In terms of relationships "fellowship," "Church fellowship," or "Gospel fellowship" define the Church. Convinced persons do not need "to idolize 'temples' and 'steeplehouses,' for the Church 'is the People which Christ is the head of.'"[31] While avoiding institutionalism, Fox thought of the Church "in terms of a kind of organism. The Church is a real functioning body of persons united in Christ who leads them."[32]

"The catholicity of the Church is to be found in the universality of its Christ . . . . The true Church can only be composed of those who are *gathered* into a purified relationship with God. Such become the Body of Christ and demonstrate what Fox calls the 'precious catholic faith.'"[33] "Gospel Order," by which individuals are *related* to one another serves as a "guide to God's constant purposes." It also provides "a check upon individualism," and it is an "effective instrument for the maintenance of a holy community. It was not to an experiment in group thinking that Fox witnessed . . . ."[34]

Worship, too, "is principally a *relationship* in which Christ is the Substance, fulfilling the doctrine and abrogating the symbol." The Church that "meets in Jesus' Name" is prepared to wait "for Wisdom, Counsel, and understanding, that by it they may be *ordered* and *directed* in His holy service and business."[35]

Arthur Roberts summarizes by stating that "the Church, in Fox's concept, presents itself before the world in these ways:

"(1) It is a *Gospel fellowship* which brings Restored individuals together by the experience of a common Christ. It is this which gives unity of Spirit and enables an outward recognition of those gathered in the New Covenant. The universality of Christ gives the Church its catholicity, and the gathered fellowship is His visible Body.

"(2) It is a *Gospel Order*" whereby "the Apostolic pattern" serves as a "historical basis and guide for revealed Authority," checks individualism and formulates "a universal basis for the Church which was endangered by incipient congregationalism," and aims to bring to bear "the leadership of Christ" on both personal problems and disputes in particular, and the "business affairs of the Church" in general.

"(3) It is a *holy community*" that demonstrates "the Restored nature of its members devotionally" through its worship, "which claims the Inspiration of the Spirit." Its "communion with Christ" is not tied to any outward symbol. Ethically it offers Testimony for Christ by responsibly witnessing to need wherever it encounters it. It emphasizes marriage "as a sanctifying ordinance of God" that is "guided by the Church," with special attention given to children "as a heritage of the Lord."

"(4) It is a *fellowship of evangelism* in which the apostolate rests especially upon the ministers who are called out of the common walks of life to speak words of reconciliation. The ministers are distinctly called of God. They may receive voluntary support in their public service." Their ordination by God, not by man, "is recognized and guarded by the Church."[36]

The Church in History

Unlike the false church that had arisen since the apostles' days, the true Church was being freshly *gathered again* in Fox's time in a radical and decisive way. In eschatological terms present and future are fused by Fox in such expressions as "the Lord is risen and rising," "come and coming," and the everlasting Gospel is being "received and receiving." "A particularly apt expression, showing the pentecostal nature of this mass movement, reads 'in this Day of the Lamb's Power.'"[37]

"There is a kind of realized eschatology in Fox's concept of the Church gathered in the Name of Jesus. In the realization of Christ's real Presence in the world, both in judgment upon apostasy and in direct Leadership of the Elect . . . . The true Church is out in the open again." It is no longer in the wilderness, and "fires and faggots can no longer suppress it . . . . After the long night of apostasy, Christ has come to Teach his People himself."[38]

Ministry as Instruments of God

Since the chapters of the *Apology* on Ministry and Worship are among the high points of Barclay's presentation and have an easily understood developmental logic, the treatment here will be brief. Quotations will be kept to a minimum, and only those that demonstrate the articulating points will be used.

"He who gathers Christians also provides among them ministers, and teachers . . . to watch over, instruct them, and maintain them in an animated, refreshed, and powerful condition. Their call is verified in the hearts of their brethren, and the seals of their apostleship are the awareness of the Life and Power passing through them . . . ." By this "true substance of a call to the ministry, a minister genuinely succeeds to the Virtue, Life, and Power which the Apostles had." No "ceremony of ordination, or the laying on of hands" is necessary. *[191]*

This "living succession" *[183, 184, 217]* is necessary for a true Christian ministry. It is impossible for "a lifeless institution" to "produce a living succession." *[184]* Not only will it retain its "lifelessness, barrenness, and dryness" but "all manner of other evils" will follow. *[178]* "Under the New Covenant the ministry ought to be more spiritual, the way more certain, and the access to the Lord more easy." *[180]*

"Those who do not agree with us" maintain that "a minister: (a) must not be a fool (b) must be schooled in languages, philosophy, and theology." They add, almost as an afterthought, that "(c) he must be favored by the grace of God." *[192]* They regard the "call" as a "sort of supererogation," *[181]* and consider "ordination" as not only necessary but virtually indispensable. *[191]*

On the other hand, "we take natural ability and lack of idiocy for granted," and consider scholarly learning unnecessary, although occasionally learnedness can concur with Grace. But it is Grace that "we consider . . . absolutely indispensable." *[192]* "The way in which Christ helps, assists, and works with us is by Grace," and without it a Christian is "a hypocrite and a pretender." It is by the Grace of Christ that "the whole body [is] joined and knit together," each part functions properly, and the Body grows "and upbuilds itself in love" (Eph. 4:16 RSV), *[193-194]* and in turn bestows "dignity . . . upon those who . . . must be fathers and instructors to others." *[193]*

Since all who are called by Christ to be "apostles, prophets, evangelists, pastors and teachers" are qualified by Grace, "no one destitute of Grace is fit for this work . . . and . . . should not be heard, received, or acknowledged as a minister of the Gospel." *[194]* And "whatever gift each of you may have received" should be used "in service to one another . . . . Are you a speaker? Speak as if you uttered oracles of God. Do you give service? Give it as in the strength which God supplies. In all things so act that the glory may be God's through Jesus Christ; to him belong glory and power for ever and ever. Amen." (1 Pet. 4:10-11 NEB) *[193-194]*

The learning necessary for a minister is the "true learning . . . [which] is the result of the inward instruction of the Spirit;" and it is by living experience that we learn "how to overcome evil and its temptations." We do so by "following the Lord, walking in his Light, and waiting daily for the direct revelation of Wisdom and Knowledge." Like the virtuous Mary "we store these heavenly and divine lessons among the good treasures of the heart" just as she preserved there "the things she observed and the sayings which she heard." [197-198]

"At the proper time," a true minister "can instruct, teach, and admonish very well" with this kind of learning. He testifies from his own experience. [198] Ours is not a hearsay ministry. When the condition of a true minister "answers the condition and experience of the faithful of old," recorded in Scripture, and he "possesses the truths that are expressed" there, by comparison whatever he could interpret in any other way is virtually worthless. What he could learn from Scripture by "his own industry . . . and knowledge of languages" without the Spirit's guidance would also lack the assurance "that he will not miss the sense of it." [199]

Summary Comments on Church and Ministry

We can combine Fox's and Barclay's theologies of the Church and of ministry up to a point. That point is the matter of "visibility." Both see "gathering" by the Grace of God through Jesus Christ as central to the Church's formation, and, when supplemented by "calling," central to some extent for its function. Both agree on Presence as vital to the true Church. Fox's phrasing, "Christ has come to teach his people himself," sums this up as a dialogic relationship between a living Lord and His followers.

This Christ who is both a prophet and more than a prophet guides His people in all their efforts to know the will of God for them both individually and collectively. As the Righteous One of Israel He sanctifies this New Israel. By His Light He not only convicts but convinces and converts. He brings His faithful followers to a new birth and a new life. "Visibility" for Fox is the visibility of a Grace-gathered community that is faithful in worship and in righteousness and service. While a "spiritual fellowship" has no empirical visibility of its own, the subordination of it to its heavenly Lord, the holiness of its members, and the charitableness of their works are not merely *signs* that the Church exists, but the very conditions for its continuance.

Barclay's "visible Church," no matter how carefully he hedges it and how well he relates it to the companion "invisible

Church," cannot escape some minimal institutionalization. The "visible Church" professes people and admits them into membership. It legislates. It disciplines. And the quality of these acts is somewhat different than those of a Church that makes no claims for itself but seeks only to be ready to do God's will and to be faithful in executing it.

Instead of stressing a visible institution, Fox speaks of a heavenly Mother for the Church, whose habitation is in the Jerusalem that is from above, not the earthly city. Barclay's "invisible Church," to be sure, is the Kingdom of the beloved Son of God. Persons are "translated" [i.e., "transported"] into this heaven-like community and "dwell" there. But some of their neighbors have not "joined" a "particular church." In fact, they may never have heard of Christ.

When we turn to ministry, however, Barclay's derivation of it from various gifts of Grace, and its unmediated inspiration by the Spirit of Christ, have definite advantages. The evanescent quality and transient commitment engendered by Fox's ad hoc and on-the-spot "ordinations" by the Spirit of Christ are avoided. And although "offices" in the early Church were more nearly "functions" in our terminology than "positions with specific job descriptions," they were definite enough to fix responsibilities. Several "offices" might concur in one person, but there was no "will-of-the-wispishness" about what was expected of that person.

Even vocal ministry—a responsibility that *no Christian* should shun—nevertheless was a gift possessed in greater degree by some. They could be said to have a "vocation" to it. But the vocation was demonstrated by gifts that could be "discerned" by all. No academically learned skills were basic, and appointment did not exclude others from their duties as Christian ministers.

"What makes a man a minister, pastor, or teacher in the Church of Christ?" It is the "inward Power and Virtue of the Spirit of God." The Grace of God "will not only call him, but in some measure purify and sanctify him . . . [And] he must be able to speak from living experience." *[178-179]* I would add, that he ought to be in readiness to become the obedient instrument of divine purposes, and minister of the Love of Christ.

Notes to Chapter 4

Italic figures in brackets within the text refer to page numbers in *Barclay's Apology in Modern English*.

1. Lewis Benson, *Catholic Quakerism* (published by the author, 1966), p. 36.
2. Fr. Yves Congar, O.P., *Lay People in the Church*, transl. by Donald Attwater, rev. by the author (Westminster, Md.: Newman, 1965), p. 28.
   It is significant that in speaking from a church that has traditionally been defined largely in terms of the clergy, the book is "a response at the doctrinal level to the need for giving the laity its full place" (p. 343); nonetheless Fr. Congar sees the Church "under the two aspects" of "institution" and "community of the faithful." (p. 37)
3. Joseph A. Fitzmyer, S.J., "Pauline Theology," *Jerome Biblical Commentary* (Englewood Cliffs, N.J.: Prentice-Hall, 1968), 79:149.
4. "It is said that Luther was the first to make the distinction" between the Church as "visible" on the one hand and "invisible" on the other, "but the other Reformers recognized and also applied it to the Church." There were considerable differences, it might be added, in the way in which the "invisibility" was interpreted – Louis Berkhof, *Systematic Theology* (London: Banner of Truth Trust, 1959), pp. 565ff.
   In Berkhof's opinion "good definitions of the visible and invisible Church may be found in the Westminster Confession." p. 567
5. In Luther's usage the "outward bodily church" and the "inner spiritual church" were "carefully discriminated, but not separated . . . [like] body and soul in man." Reinhold Seeberg, *Textbook of the History of Doctrines*, transl. by Charles E. Hay (Grand Rapids, Mich.: Baker, 1964), vol. 2, p. 291.
6. Lewis Benson, *Catholic Quakerism*, p. 39
7. *Ibid*. p. 37.
8. Lewis Benson, "The Early Quaker Vision of the Church," *Quaker Religious Thought*, II:1(Spring, 1960):16, 7.
9. Lewis Benson, *Catholic Quakerism*, pp. 35-36.
10. Lewis Benson, *Quaker Religious Thought*, II:1(Spring 1960):8.
11. Lewis Benson, *Catholic Quakerism*, p. 34.
12. George Fox, *Journal*, Bi-Centenary edition (London, 1891), II:436-437.
13. George Fox, *Works of George Fox*, 8 vols. (Philadelphia: M.T.C. Gould, 1931) 8:174 and 7:228-229 and 6:642.
14. Fox, *Journal*, Bi-Centenary edition, II:122.
15. Although the *Jerusalem Bible* note on Jn. 4:23-24 interprets this verse in liturgical terms, it does so metaphorically, stating that "from now on Christians are able to enter this Kingdom and live there a life that is a eucharistic liturgy."
16. The Fox quote is from *Journal*, Bi-Centenary edition, II:422-423. The *Jerusalem Bible* note is again of interest: "The Spirit who makes a new creature of man (Jn. 3:5) is also the inspiring principle of the new worship of God. This worship is 'in truth' because it is the only worship that meets the conditions revealed by God through Jesus."
17. A note in the *Jerusalem Bible* sees the descent of Jerusalem as "renewal in these present, messianic times; the transformation of humanity by an act of God." See also Fox, *Works of George Fox*, 4:186; Fox, *Journal*, Bi-Centenary edition, I:348; and manuscript Aa 5,110G.157 *MS Catalogue of George Fox* (compiled 1694-1697).
18. Fox, *Works of George Fox*, 4:186 and 4:243.
19. *Ibid.*, 5:335 and 7:157.
20. Donald S. Nesti, C.S.Sp., "Early Quaker Ecclesiology," *Quaker Religious Thought*, vol. 18, no. 1(Autumn '78):20-21.
21. Arthur Roberts, "George Fox's Concept of the Church," Ph.D. Thesis, Boston University, 1954.
22. *Ibid.*, p. 196.
23. *Ibid.*, p. 47, quoting Fox, *Journal*, Bi-Centenary edition, I:26.

24 *Ibid.*, pp. 85-86, quoting *Works of George Fox,* 5:201 and 6:23.
25 *Ibid.*, p. 86, quoting *Works of George Fox,* 5:89.
26 Roberts, p. 106. Cf. also Lewis Benson, *Catholic Quakerism,* p. 38: "the spiritual home God intended . . ." and 43: "everything . . . spoiled and corrupted by disobedience would be Restored again by Christ and his saints."
27 *Ibid.*, pp. 117, 119, quoting *Works of George Fox,* 6:68. Cf. also 6:38-77.
28 *Ibid.*, pp. 119, 121, for which the basis is Fox, *Works of George Fox,* 3:76-77, 191-192.
29 Roberts, pp. 119, 121.
30 *Ibid.*, p. 123.
31 *Ibid.*, p. 123, quoting George Fox, *Journal,* revised edition by John L. Nickalls (Cambridge: University Press, 1952), p. 107.
32 Roberts, p. 127. Based on Emerson Shideler, "Spiritual Ecclesiology," p. 40. Shideler states that "the Church was not only the communion of saints in idea: it was the communion of saints in fact for Fox."
33 *Ibid.*, pp. 128-129. *Italics* added. Quoting *Works of George Fox,* 5:449.
34 *Ibid.*, p. 146.
35 *Ibid.*, pp. 147-149. *Italics* added.
36 *Ibid.*, pp. 172-173.
37 *Ibid.*, p. 174.
38 *Ibid.*, pp. 175-176.

Chapter 5

WORSHIP IN SPIRIT AND IN TRUTH

The chapters on Worship, Ministry, Baptism, and Communion in the *Apology* are so clearly and logically developed that no guidance is needed to follow or understand them. Modern biblical scholarship and current research into early church history lend considerable support both to the particular scriptural citations used and the argument that Barclay develops from them. Regrettably, although the resolution of the issues they raise is vital to any genuine recovery of apostolic faith and practice, other Christians have largely ignored their testimony.

With that in mind, enough Barclay will be quoted here to indicate his awareness of problems that continue to plague both Friends and the ecumenical movement. Then, after a look at the current Quaker situation, worship will be approached in the generic sense, to see if that will shed some light on the significance of particular aspects of the kind of worship usually thought of as distinctively Quaker.

The Current Situation

In some Quaker circles, the pastoral system and "programmed worship" – with hymns, responsive readings, and sermons often following a printed program – are now a century old. The Quaker justification for adaptation to pastoral leadership is usually found in the Richmond documents of 1892 and 1897. Extrinsic factors owed much to Methodist evangelization in a frontier environment.[1] Some additional rootage can be claimed for the pastoral system in the traveling ministry unique to

Friends in the seventeenth century, although the evangelization of that period usually resulted in "settled meetings" whose worship was based on silent expectant waiting.

Silence is by no means a monopoly of unprogrammed meetings. Periods of silence are frequent in pastoral meetings, although the presuppositions behind these periods may vary widely. They range from a token silence in which the vacuity some feel is "wall-papered over" with meditative organ music, to genuine depth in which the reality of the Presence of Christ is sensed. Where the latter is the case, vocal ministry is apt to arise from the congregation as well as the pulpit.

Team ministry is another approach in a few larger meetings. While it may not be the whole answer to the difficult problem of reconciling programmed and unprogrammed types of worship, it most certainly challenges the mono-pastoral emphasis on solely pulpit-centered ministry. It is increasingly common for both programmed and unprogrammed worship to take place in the same building, and frequently under the care of the same monthly meeting. Be it said, too, that pastoral meetings usually demonstrate the early Quaker concern for outreach/evangelism. It seems to be easier for an unprogrammed meeting to become ingrown and unreceptive to newcomers, and there is generally almost an embarrassment about undertaking any kind of evangelism/outreach.

By and large the pastoral meetings place a stronger emphasis on all aspects of mission—foreign mission as well as home mission—and are often involved in the service-type to meet community needs as well. Unfortunately the unprogrammed meetings, while usually strong in social action, are usually remiss in adequately proclaiming the Gospel as an accompaniment to and undergirding of their social action. And their vocal ministry often reflects a shallowness in knowledge of Scripture.

Teaching ministry may also be less frequent in unprogrammed meetings for worship. One of the strengths of all kinds of Quakers, however, is their respect for education and the printed word. This tends to make the religious education of children flourish wherever agreement on curriculum can be reached and volunteers are available.

The difficulty with which one generalizes about anything as characteristic of one Quaker group or another is a mark of the rapprochement that is taking place between all of them. It is a hopeful sign that they are being mutually renewed by the closer encounter and cooperation developing in recent years, but theological thought that would provide a basis for genuine reconciliation of pastoral and nonpastoral approaches is still elusive. Nonetheless, some pointers (guidelines would be too pretentious a term) can be found in the following paragraphs.

Dorlan Bales willingly admits that the analysis he has made is more pragmatic than revealed.[2] It speaks of a "three-stage approach" to a "semiprogrammed worship model" several congregations have been using. It sees "equipping others for all sorts of ministry, including vocal ministry in worship" as "an important aim" for "ministry and worship committees, including pastoral ministers." He outlines three stages: (1) "A time of transition ... into a deeper awareness of Christ's Presence" facilitated for some "by quiet waiting on the Lord; for others by singing and sharing of community concerns." (2) "A time of vocal ministry" by "one or more persons who have ... come prepared to share ... if the Spirit allows it." (3) "A significant amount of unstructured time in which the worshipers meditate upon the songs and spoken ministry which have been shared, and upon the store of need and gratitude which they bring to worship." From this, spoken messages will often develop from the congregation.

"In this approach the sermon is not the centerpiece or climax of worship, but a means of preparing for and encouraging the deeper level of worship which follows." Dorlan Bales sees beginning-era worship as a "tension between quiet listening and vocal ministry," and something that can be "recaptured" if we achieve "a better balance in our worship between our efforts to communicate, and quiet inward receptivity."

However, as far as I know, the only "balance" that early Friends sought was to distribute the visits of the Friends most gifted in ministry in such a way that they "would not all arrive in heaps." What is more, the relationship between speech and silence was not one of tension, but the silence served as a waiting period in which one might be called to speak under direct inspiration and guidance. And it is hardly likely that the early itinerant ministers viewed their role as stimulating others to meditate.

A "gathered meeting" should move beyond meditation to holy expectancy, a time of passive yet alert receptivity to God's will and charge, received through both the indwelling Presence of Christ and His Presence in the midst of the worshipers. At that level of gatheredness, faith prompts the belief that worshipers will be told what they are to do or say, for in Fox's words: "Christ has come to teach his People himself," without human mediation. In the final analysis, the *only* stimulus, inspiration, and norm is Christ, who presides and guides and inspires through the Spirit. Those who have come to learn from and *follow* Him are confident that He will show them the Way Himself, and that what He shows them, and what He bids them do, will so transform the quality of their lives that they will become New Creatures, citizens of heaven and children of God, sojourning on earth for a time.

Are such thoughts more of a projection of my own feelings than an objective analysis of the theology behind Quaker worship? Certain affirmations regarding "public worship," in the Richmond Declaration of Faith (1887) seem to be even more precise on these matters and offer a more concise parallel statement:

> "We recognize the value of silence, not as an end, but as a means toward the attainment of the end; a silence, not of listlessness or of vacant musing, but of holy expectation before the Lord. [We unite as] adopted children through faith in the Lord Jesus Christ . . . in the worship of Almighty God, to wait upon Him for the renewal of our strength, for communion one with another, for the edification of believers in the exercise of various spiritual gifts, and for the declaration of the glad tidings of salvation . . . . This worship depends not upon numbers. Where two or three are gathered together in the name of Christ there is a church, and Christ, the living Head, in the midst of them. Through His mediation, without the necessity for any inferior instrumentality, is the Father to be approached and reverently worshipped . . . .
>
> As it is the prerogative of the Great Head of the church alone to select and call the ministers of His Gospel, so we believe that . . . by the immediate operations of the Holy Spirit . . . both the gift and the qualification to exercise it must be derived immediately from Him; and that, as in the primitive church, so now also, He confers spiritual gifts upon women as well as upon men . . . .
>
> The true disciple will be found still sitting at the feet of Jesus, listening that he may learn, and learning that he may obey.

Unfortunately, much of the worship and ministry in pastoral meetings is still dependent upon other denominational groupings for its current rationale and any potential renewal. However, conferences on ministry for Quaker pastors have been introduced, and syncretistic tendencies are being ameliorated (at least for the pastors of Friends United Meeting) by the establishment of an American Quaker seminary, the Earlham School of Religion, which is now in its third decade. In the initial stages Quaker pastors were seldom formally trained, but in recent years they have tended to train in the seminaries of other denominations; or, pastors of other denominations have frequently been called to Quaker pulpits.

These and other facts call for a reexamination of the nature and content of traditional Quaker worship. All the Quaker subspecies are reassessing their beginnings as well as the extra-denominational tensions still being exerted upon them. There is an effort to sort out what is authentically Quaker, and to determine whether it can and ought to be preserved and built upon; preferably by all of the subdenominational groupings acting together, or at least in concert.

While the problem for unprogrammed meetings has been dissipation more frequently than syncretism, they are by no means exempt from outside influences. Some have been subjected to unitarian and humanist influences. While others have resolutely preserved a Christian basis, unfortunately it is sometimes stilted and dated, or quietistic.

As far as I am aware, there is no such thing as a unitarian or nonchristian pastoral meeting. But that does not protect pastored meetings from overly pietistic or overly liberal approaches, or the inroads of American cultural religion, or some of the imbalances peculiar to the mainstream churches that have affected them most. They sometimes exhibit at one and the same time greater sophistication than the groups from which they borrow, while they display some of the same faults to an even greater degree.[3]

Before leaving efforts toward a common theological rationale for worship and the tentative pointers that have already been enunciated, it needs to be said that one of the most difficult claims for which to maintain credibility today is Barclay's assertion that unprogrammed worship is the *only* worship that is "worship in Spirit and in Truth." (Jn. 4:23-24) Or, for that matter, the claim that unprogrammed worship is the *only way* in which "worship in Spirit and in Truth" could be practiced.

Yet surprising support for that possibility seems to be implied in some current research. Furthermore, since the third century there has been no other attempt of such magnitude to implement the role of Christ as Prophet (and more than a prophet) as the basis for worship. With these facts in mind, let us have a look at some current mainstream assertions on the subject of worship.

Worship in Ecumenical Perspective

Horton Davies, who has offered an empathic look (in very brief compass) at the history and meaning of Christian worship, finds "the greater part of the variety" to be "due to historical and geographical factors."[4] He sees the Baptist and Congregationalist willingness to rely "upon the direct leading of the Holy Spirit in free or extemporaneous prayer" as a "Puritan protest against the *Book of Common Prayer*" and considers the "immanental, immediate, Spirit-inspired worship of the Society of Friends . . . the final step in this movement."[5] Furthermore, he sees "the temple and the synagogue and their liturgies" as forming the natural background of worship in the Apostolic Church.[6]

Horton Davies makes no mention of the gift-oriented ministry described in the New Testament. Although it is not portrayed with as much detail elsewhere in the epistolary literature as it is in 1 Corinthians 12 and 14, that kind of ministry does seem to be implied even in a work usually considered to be quite late, that is 1 Peter (cf. 1 Pet. 4:10). There are also relics of an earlier and simpler nonclerical ministry in Matthew 13:17 that preserve a distinction between "prophets and righteous men."[7] Monsignor Ronald Knox effectively ridiculed and condemned all modern grace-derived ministries by indiscriminately labeling them "enthusiasm." His mixed bag lumped extremist and legitimate varieties together without any real differentiation.[8]

As early as 1660, Samuel Fisher, who was an ordained Anglican with an Oxford M.A. before he became a Quaker, protested against this kind of treatment. It not only results in what would be called "stereotyping" today, but smothers even varieties that are at all adequately examined with a sort of variegated tar and feathering. Fisher stated that priests of the English Church reject and condemn gift-oriented ministry "under the several respective names of schism, schismatical, schismatics; heretical, heresy, heretics; lying-spirit; delusion, deluders; fanatical, fanaticism, fanatics; enthusiastical, enthusiasm, enthusiasts; dreams, dreamers; fictions, figments; Quakers, and whatever other ignominious terms any ungodly scoffers can invent."[9]

The Lutheran exegete Ernst Käsemann, who pointed out the significance of Matthew 13:17, above, nonetheless revives this belittling Reformation label even for the worship described in the canonical New Testament. Can such a pejorative tilting of the evidence be countenanced in an ecumenical age? The stubborn fact remains that traditional Quaker worship is the closest to what is actually described in the Pauline epistles, 1 Corinthians 14:26-33 and elsewhere, as the *Interpreter's Bible* duly noted in Clarence Tucker Craig's exegesis and John Short's exposition of those passages. Both scholars, be it added, are non-Quakers!

The fluid nature of "forms" in early Christian worship is noted by Horton Davies, who says they "did not crystallize until the fourth and fifth centuries."[10] Fr. Josef A. Jungmann, S.J., the revered author of *The Mass of the Roman Rite,* states that "Stephen the Protomartyr shed his blood for the concept that the liturgy of the Old Testament and the cult connected with the Temple at Jerusalem had to cease and that a new sort of worship which is inward and spiritual must take its place."[11]

"The oldest celebration of the Eucharist took the form of a meal at least in some places and at least for a few decades . . . . The great change which occurred in liturgical practice, the greatest perhaps in the whole course of the history of the Mass, was the abandonment of the meal as a setting for the Mass . . . by the end of the first century." Nevertheless, Fr. Jungmann says, the question: "What did the celebration of the Eucharist look like during the time of the Apostles? . . . is a question to which we cannot give a definite answer."[12]

Some evaluations of worship today see Protestantism as having returned to continuity with antecedent synagogue worship and Roman Catholics as having modified temple worship. Thus the primary formative influences have been historical and cultural, and to some extent accidental, rather than any conscious reformation in terms of the radical changes foreseen by Christ for the era of the New Covenant. Furthermore, very few objective criteria are available for use in assaying the authenticity of one type of worship against another. Most views of worship in ecumenical perspective simply see various generic forms in use in different World Communions. They make no effort to derive them from Scripture or to find a biblical basis that would justify them.

A liturgist simply sees all worship in liturgical terms. A Free-Churchman allows room for the spiritual inspiration of the prayers, choice of Bible readings, and sermon topic; but he considers the basic sermon-oriented structure to be beyond questioning. A Lutheran-Reformed synthesis takes a both/and approach and declares the word rightly preached and the sacrament rightly administered to be the fundamental criteria for all worship.

The Church Year with its appointed seasons and festivals, together with a lectionary on a three-year cycle of set readings from Scripture, rigidly define the framework of worship for a large band of liturgically oriented communions and some middle Protestants as well. Within that band there is some flexibility in the number and kind of festivals and some options on Scripture texts. But almost all of the approaches that have been mentioned have been historically, magisterially, or cooperatively determined. They are not derived from any direct theological evaluation of New Testament evidence, nor do they even concede that relevant for anything but simple "proofs" for a few of the components.

Barclay clearly recognizes that paucity of biblical evidence may have been a major factor in this rather haphazard development of Christian worship. "Christ has particularly promised his blessing upon those who assemble together in his Name," [280] "however, no set form of worship under the purer administration of the New Covenant is prescribed for his children by Jesus Christ, the Author of the Christian religion. He merely tells them that the worship which is now to be performed is spiritual, and in the Spirit. It should be especially observed that the only order or command [of Christ] pertaining to worship in the entire New Testament, other than the injunction to follow the Spirit, is the general instruction to meet together." [263]

Even a cursory examination of the nature of worship brings the vast differences in basic types into view. It is also seen how most practitioners, including Friends, have the conviction that their particular type of worship is the right one. But why are there so many different forms? What explanation is there for these differences? What criteria are available for objective comparison or theological evaluation? The answer that we are given by one authority[13] is that we are dealing with a phenomenon so ancient and so universal that its origins cannot be documented. They can only be implied from the study of primitive religions and by sociological and philosophical comparison of the various forms found in modern religions. And even this approach is questioned by some.

One of the latest encyclopedias of theology, *Sacramentum Mundi*, has a little over two pages on "Worship," although there are nearly twenty on "Liturgy."[14] In the article on liturgy[15] there is no situating of "liturgical worship" as one *phylum* (to borrow a term from scientific taxonomy), or major family of worship types. The article opens by saying that "the word *leitourgia* in classical Greek means a function *(ergon)* undertaken on behalf of the people *(laos)*: fitting out a ship, preparing a feast, or doing any public service." Obviously, the fact that the function is "undertaken on behalf of the people" implies a relatively passive role for them.

The other *Sacramentum Mundi* article on "Worship" immediately delimits its task. "This article is an endeavor to explain the notion of worship, not to give an account of its various forms." Turning to Judeo-Christian worship as understood theologically, the article notes that it was worship that *created* a people of God, and that worship renews them again and again.[16] For Christians "salutary participation includes love of God and of the neighbor." Furthermore "the fraternal unity of all worshippers" as an "essential element" was stated (understandably in Eucharistic terms) as far back as Augustine. "Real participation . . . proves its fruitfulness in the works of mercy, in the efforts to reshape the world in a way more worthy of man, so that the whole Christian life has the character of worship . . . ." Curiously many Friends, although they eschew sacramental rites, come to a conclusion stated in closely similar wording: "All of life should be sacramental."

An older work published in 1912,[17] when serious study of primitive religions was just beginning and Comparative Religion as a discipline was only half a century old, states: "Worship may be defined as the acknowledgment by some formal act of mind or body, or both, of God's supreme dominion, or (among pagans) of the exalted power of some divine or semi-divine being."

A few years later, Rudolf Otto was to "patiently seek to penetrate the obscurity which veils the mental processes of primitive and uncivilized man," as the 1912 Coleman article (already referred to) had defined the task of determining origins of religion. However, Otto was less occupied with determining origins or the nature of worship than he was with the nature of God. His phrase the "wholly other" has become an accepted part of the vocabulary of religion. Nonetheless, the nature of worship did not escape his attention altogether.

The eighth of his 13 appendices to *The Idea of the Holy*[18] is called "Silent Worship," and is an analysis of traditional Quaker worship. "It is," he says, "the most spiritual form of divine service which has ever been practiced, and contains an element which no form of worship ought to be without . . . ." In it, the silence is "primarily not so much a dumbness in the presence of Deity, as an awaiting His coming . . . ." He sees that this "waiting" may also "have been a direct 'numinous' experience as well." In that case "silence became a Sacrament," and the consummation of a Sacrament "is the achievement of unity, i.e., fellowship and *Communion.*" Thus, he says: "The Silent worship of the Quakers is in fact a realization of Communion in both senses of the word—inward oneness and fellowship of the indi-vidual with invisible present Reality and the mystical union of many individuals with one another."

Rudolf Otto did not think that "Silent Worship, in the fully formed character in which the Quakers practise it," would be possible in a large "Church," but "only within the narrower limits of a more intimate 'Brotherhood of the Spirit.'" Nonetheless, he viewed that worship in the highest terms, seeing "the plainest inward kinship" between "the Quaker Meeting and the Roman Catholic Mass: *Both* are solemn religious observances of a numinous and sacramental character, *both* are communion, *both* [italics his] exhibit alike an inner straining not only 'to realize the presence' of God, but to attain to a degree of oneness with Him."

One cannot fault Otto for his emphasis on silence and the lack of any dimension of prophetic expectation. His Quaker source, Violet Hodgkin's *Silent Worship: The Way of Wonder*, as her title suggests, viewed worship in that way. While the relationship between the mystical and the prophetic has yet to be satisfactorily determined, the prophetic aspect of worship in George Fox's understanding of it has been recovered by Lewis Benson. Much as I value the recovery of the prophetic dimension of worship and see it as both felicitous and necessary, I hope that will not lead to any sort of denial of the centrality of Communion in traditional Quaker worship.

In addition to the "holy expectancy" (with which one tract characterized the attitude of gathered worshipers) an explicit reference to the lordship of Christ is needed. This should spell out His role as initiator, governor, and inspirer of all that takes place. In addition to the fellowship and communion (*koinonia* can be translated both ways) that are part of the expectation, worship is fulfilled in witness and service. The will of Christ for His people and their obedience not only constitute the basis for the Church, but the basis for the Church's worship as well. A New Jersey Friend, Charles Trafford, once used the expressive imagery that in meeting for worship we extend our hand toward Christ, and in doing so we hope that He will take it and show us the next step.

In concluding this commentary, which serves as preparation and background for the reading of Barclay's own description of "unprogrammed worship"—still the best available treatment in depth after more than 300 years—some comments of my own on today's context may be in order. These remarks have to be made with full cognizance of the difficulty of interpreting unprogrammed and unpastored worship to others and to Friends as well, now that three quarters of the Friends in America (and perhaps a higher percentage worldwide) use programmed worship, commonly (although not exclusively) conducted by a pastor.

This is no condemnation of pastors, who have labored diligently and conscientiously and who in many respects preserve more of the original Quaker emphasis in other areas than those who still use the shared ministry. Yet it is difficult to counter the impression that outsiders have that all Friends will have pastors "as soon as they can afford them." There is something more serious than this distortion, however. It is the fact that without worship centered on Christ as Prophet, Lord, and Mediator, testimony for Christ would lack the witness that a church without a lay-clerical dichotomy, without liturgy or sacraments, and without worship conceived of as in any way "undertaken on behalf of" the worshipers, can not only function, but has managed to function successfully for more than three centuries.

In that time, and with only a miniscule percentage of the world's Christians practicing it, that form of worship has been a major factor in fomenting constructive social change; and it has made a significant contribution to Christian spirituality as well. In the religious world it is an endangered species that deserves prayerful support from all varieties of Friends. This totally shared ministry not only emphasizes patient and quiet waiting for guidance, but also the ultimate in responsibility. Where Christ's leading comes directly to individuals in a gathered group, neither responsibility for the worship itself nor obedience to its demands can be sloughed off onto the pastor. And when a particular individual receives inspiration and guidance from his/her Lord, it is difficult to escape the task laid upon her/him or to pass it along to someone else.

A final analysis, which deserves attention before reading Barclay's chapter on worship, is one found in *A Dictionary of Liturgy and Worship* edited by J. G. Davies.[19] In spite of the book's title, there is no article on "Worship." There is a 25-page article on "Liturgies," which classifies them into fifteen types and uses a definition broad enough to include Pentecostal, Plymouth Brethren, Seventh-day Adventist, Jehovah's Witnesses, Congregationalist, and Baptist forms within its compass. Each of these forms also has a separate article called "Pentecostal Worship," "Plymouth Brethren Worship," etc. Both types of treatment are excellent, and it is no belittling of their contents to say that it is difficult to understand why many of these forms of worship were included under "Liturgies."

As extended a definition as that inclusiveness implies, fortunately it does not seem to have been broad enough to warrant the term "Quaker Liturgy." There does appear, however, an excellent article on "Quaker Worship" by Maurice Creasey, who served as director of studies (1953-1977) at Woodbrooke in the interdenominational Selly Oak Colleges grouping in Birmingham, England.[20] With some irony, the article falls alphabetically between "Quadragesima" and "Quinquagesima."

Maurice Creasey states, in part: "Ecumenical discussion recognizes the existence of three broad types of worship, often referred to as 'altar-centered,' 'pulpit-centered,' and 'waiting upon the Spirit.' Traditional Quaker worship, with its abandonment of prearranged form, ordained ministry, and sacraments, is then seen as the extreme example of this third type. Its true character is positively determined, however, by the full seriousness with which it witnesses to the reality behind the words, 'Where two or three are gathered together in my name, there am I in the midst . . . .'

"Such a group seeks to *offer*, in attentive and expectant waiting, its present experiences, needs, confessions, thanksgivings, and intercessions. It *awaits* a word . . . [which may include] prayer, exhortation, reflection upon experience, exposition of a biblical passage or theme. The keynote . . . is . . . the profoundly simple intention, by a gathered group, of opening itself to the presence of Christ, to the implications of the discovery that Christ's presence in the Spirit requires no other mediation and is that by which isolation is overcome and communion is experienced . . . .

"Both for the Society of Friends and for the Christian Church as a whole, this mode of worship today raises far-reaching questions. If it is not, as the early Friends claimed, the *only* form of worship appropriate to the new covenant dispensation, what is it? Is it simply a mode which appeals to certain temperaments? Or is it an emphasis – even an exaggeration – justified so long as it is balanced or offset by other emphases? Or is it possible that it represents an essential ingredient or dimension of worship which, historically, found separate expression in conscious opposition to others? To express the matter otherwise, is it possible to think that, with other forms, it points beyond itself and them towards an understanding of the fullness of worship appropriate to today?"

At least generic claims to apostolicity for the type of worship Barclay describes would seem to have an edge for priority over those that are "pulpit-centered" or "altar-centered." This seems to be the evidence from the various writers on the history of worship who have been cited in the present chapter. Some of them have been willing to say more and to attribute unique qualities to unprogrammed worship.

Notes to Chapter 5

Italic figures in brackets within the text refer to page numbers in *Barclay's Apology in Modern English*.

1   The section called "About the Apology" in *Barclay's Apology in Modern English* calls attention to the earlier and somewhat deeper influence of Quakerism on John Wesley and Methodism.
2   In a Quaker Theological Discussion Group paper presented at Barnesville, Ohio, in July 1982, and published in *Quaker Life* Series 24, No. 1 (Jan-Feb '83):7-9.
3   An "unholy trinity" of professionalism, consumerism, and theatricalism is dealt with in my Response to E. Glenn Hinson's "Voluntarism and Holy Obedience," pp. 25-35 of *Prayer and Holy Obedience in a War-Wracked World*, the papers from a Southern Baptist-Quaker Colloquy at Berea College, Berea, Ky., ed. by Glenn Igleheart (Atlanta: Home Mission Board, 1982).
4   Horton Davies, *Christian Worship: Its History and Meaning* (New York: Abingdon, 1957), p. 118.
5   Davies, op. cit., p. 65.
6   *Ibid.*, p. 19.
7   Ernst Käsemann, "The Beginnings of Christian Theology," in *Journal for Theology and The Church*, vol. 6, "Apocalypticism," ed. by Robert W. Funk, (New York: Herder & Herder, 1969), pp. 27-28.
8   See: Dean Freiday, "Some Positive 'Enthusiasm'," *The Friends' Quarterly*, (London), vol. 16, no. 11 (July, 1970): 553-560.
9   Samuel Fisher, "Fourth Apology," in his *Collected Labors*, Folio, no. pl. or publ., 1679, p. 567.
10 Davies, op. cit., p. 25.
11 Josef A. Jungmann, S.J., *The Early Liturgy: To the Time of Gregory the Great* (London: Darton, Longman & Todd, 1959), p. 11.
12 *Ibid.*, pp. 30, 37, 38.
13 A. I. du P. Coleman, "Worship," in *The New Schaff-Herzog Encyclopedia of Religious Knowledge*, ed. by Samual Macauley Jackson (New York: Funk & Wagnalls, 1912), vol. 12, pp. 433-441.
14 Michael Schmaus, "Worship," in *Sacramentum Mundi: An Encylopedia of Theology*, ed. by Karl Rahner, S.J., with Cornelius Ernst, O.P., and Kevin Smyth (New York, Herder & Herder, 1970), vol. 6, pp. 390-392. Joseph Andreas Jungmann and Angelus Häussling, "Liturgy," in *Sacr. Mundi*, vol. 3, pp. 320-340.
15 Jungmann and Häussling, *loc. cit.*
16 The pertinent biblical passages, although uncited, are 1 Peter 2:10, Rom. 9:25, Hos. 2:23.
17 *The New Schaff-Herzog* cited above.
18 Rudolf Otto, *The Idea of the Holy* (London: Oxford, 1923). The 2nd Engl. ed. 1950, transl. from the 9th Germ. ed. added four appendices to the original nine.
19 *A Dictionary of Liturgy and Worship* ed. by J. G. Davies (New York: Macmillan, 1972) (c) by SCM Press Ltd., London.
20 Maurice A. Creasey, "Quaker Worship" in *A Dictionary of Liturgy and Worship* cited above, pp. 328-330.

Chapter 6

ORDER

"Order" has been of sufficient ecumenical significance to be coupled with "faith" as the designation of the Faith and Order movement, which subsequently became an integral part of the World Council of Churches. For most WCC "member churches" Order implies a constitutionally authorized juridical organization of some sort.

In some cases the legalistic aspects are reinforced by a body of Canon Law. In others there is a Moderator whose role is that of a sort of instantaneous supreme court, ruling on which regulations apply and how they are to be interpreted. In other churches the Moderator is the presiding presbyter who is considered first among equals.

Most institutional church organization patterns, however else they may be composed, usually include some "ordinances" or "sacraments" that Christ is claimed to have instituted. The number of these and the significance attached to them varies in different churches. For some they are nearly central, and elaborate hierarchical structures and liturgies have been built upon them. For others their relationship to church government is marginal, and they tend to be subordinated to preaching in worship.

In some the "Sacrament of Orders" forms the basis for part of this institutional structure. This Sacrament has been declared to imprint an indelible character upon the soul, and to be the means "by which spiritual power is given and grace conferred for the performance of sacred duties."[1] It is further claimed that *Ordo* (the Latin equivalent of the Greek *taxis*) "means 'rank,' whether high or low." Even this meaning was further restricted, "much as our own word 'rank' often is, to 'eminent rank' – i.e., the clerical position as distinct from that of laymen."[2] Other WCC member churches would insist upon the necessity for the "historic Episcopate" and a physical "Succession," maintained throughout the ages by the laying on of hands.

The fourth World Conference on Faith and Order at Montreal in 1963 declared that "there must be no playing of charisma and institution against one another" in viewing the Church. But since it had already asked in the same paragraph "whether God is bound to the instruments that he has given and commanded as the means of his presence," the institution and the implicit subordination of charisma to the institution are obviously taken for granted.[3] This effectively precludes discussion in terms other than these two poles. However, the discussions of "institutionless Christianity" that took place somewhere in the vicinity of the "death of God" theologies are no help either. Now that the furor has died down, one can go back comfortably, it is assumed, to claiming divine sanction for whatever has developed through the years however different the end product may be from the original starting point.

An Order That Is Qualitative

In spite of all the significance others attach to Order, Friends seem to be alone in stressing that it is *the quality of the proceedings and the relationships* – not the nature or the authoritativeness of the structure – that should be paramount in all considerations of Order. While *the four "marks"* of the Church found in the Nicene Creed – unity, holiness, catholicity, and apostolicity – *can be construed qualitatively,* they are almost always applied empirically to *the institutional aspects* of the Church. "Unity" then means organizational unification rather than oneness of mind and spirit. "Holiness" instead of being a descriptive noun becomes a sacralizing adjective: "holy Church, holy oil, holy water, holy orders." There are also "Sacred Books, sacred liturgies, sacred congregations (e.g., "of rites"), sacred ground, or a Sanctuary." "Catholicity" becomes almost wholly the universal, geographical dimension of the Church with fullness of faith and doctrine relegated to second place. "Apostolicity" becomes historical continuity rather than authentic witness.

The traditional structure of meetings that Fox established is named for the frequency with which they meet to administer church affairs – monthly, quarterly (or half-yearly) and yearly meetings. The only hierarchical aspects of these are reservation of the preparation of statements of faith and handbooks of discipline to the yearly meeting, and (although in practice, it is almost unknown) ultimate appeal to that body in disciplinary matters. Membership, however, resides in the monthly meeting, discipline begins there, and all action that does not pertain to a larger geographic area (the principal reason for having quarterly and yearly meetings) is undertaken there.

While some have tended to apply the terms "congregational" or "connectional" to these relationships, Fox would undoubtedly have resisted this. For him, the Church was primarily a people of God, who could be ordered and reordered in an almost infinite variety of ways. The same individuals could constitute a business meeting, a meeting for ministry and counsel, a meeting by professions or vocations (e.g., doctors, lawyers, writers), or be organized to give special attention to particular concerns (e.g., family matters or prison care or reform).

Each of these groups could have its own clerk or other appointed head and seldom needed "subordination" to another grouping in the modern business organization-chart sense. It might nevertheless decide or be directed to *report* to another body. However, the only "top management" would be by the celestial Lord of Assemblies. Defined geographic scope and a clear delineation of purpose were sufficient where all subordinated themselves to a risen Lord in full consciousness that it was He who had called and gathered them.

Fox insisted that this structure itself has no sacral significance. The important thing is the nature of the presuppositions behind the structure. It must not interfere in any way with the direct communication of the believer with his/her risen Lord. All present (including those under appointment) are subordinated to the will of Christ for His people. And no position or appointment confers any arbitrary authority or status. These are the significant "marks" and the essence of this understanding of Order.

In no sense can this be stretched in such a way as to view the Church as "institution," implying, as that does, a sacralized autonomy. Nevertheless, the Quaker view of the Church most certainly is not a "playing of charisma and . . . [structure] against one another." Rather the structures must be molded by and yield to the principles that Christ enunciated. For example in Mark 10:42, 44 and Luke 22:25, His final instructions before the Passover are: "You know that among the pagans their so-called rulers lord it over them, and their great men make their authority felt . . . [but] anyone who wants to become great among you must be your servant and . . . slave to all." (Jer B)

Other clues to the quality of the relationships that are appropriate for Christians are found elsewhere in the New Testament. Yet in spite of these clear injunctions, Order has been an area of theology where a great superstructure quite legalistic and institutional in tone has tended to be imposed by using juridical rather than spiritual interpretations of the relatively limited number of texts that could be bent to such purposes. This was true in spite of the fact that it was possible to interpret these juridically only by disregarding other texts that emphasized a radically different way of doing business – not only in the church but in daily life as well. Above all, this way of interpreting these passages required a complete disregard of the thrust and context of the very text that is quoted so often as support for such constructions, 1 Cor. 14:40 RSV: ". . . all things should be done decently and in order."[4]

Robert Barclay on Order

When we turn to what Robert Barclay has to say on Order, we find a reminiscence of the same generally used palmary text, 1 Cor. 14:40, but the emphasis is placed on the Spirit in which things are done rather than on a legal structure erected in imitation of civil models. His emphasis is on the Spirit being a "Spirit of order and not of confusion." *[207]* And the consequences Barclay draws are altogether different from those we have been describing from other ecclesiastical conceptions of Order: "In a true Church of Christ, gathered together by God, not only into belief in the principles of Truth, but also into the Power and Life and Spirit of Christ, it is the Spirit of God that is the Orderer, Ruler, and Governor – not only in general but in each particular matter. Whenever the believers are assembled to wait upon God for adoration and worship, those whom the Spirit sets apart for the ministry are thus ordained by God and admitted to the ministry. Their mouths are opened by the divine power and influence of the Spirit, and words are given to them by which they exhort, reprove, and instruct with virtue and with power. Their brethren cannot do otherwise than hear them, receive them, and also give them honor for the sake of their work." *[210]*

"Some want a chief bishop or pope to be first in the church and to rule and be an over-all prince." *[207]* "Others are opposed to all precedence among pastors and constitute their subordination not in persons but in powers." *[208]* "Recent history is full of the tragedies resulting from this spiritual and ecclesiastical monarchy and commonwealth . . . . Many of the orders and forms which they use are not even mentioned in the Scripture." [209]

"In opposition to all this mass of formality and the innumerable orders, rules, and forms of church government, we maintain that the substance is the principal thing to be sought. It is the Power, Virtue, and Spirit that are to be known and waited for. These are the things which bring unity to all of the different names and offices used in the Scripture." [209] The Spirit "leads us and as many as follow it into such a becoming and decent order as is appropriate for the Church of God" [207]; and "the ministry is not monopolized by a certain kind of men set aside as clergy." [210]

Clericalization

Since the whole history of clericalization is seldom synthesized in a single place, a brief survey of the progressive episcopalization, then clericalization, and finally hierarchicalization of the Church may be appropriate here. In dealing with the question of the later editing of Paul's letters, Leander Keck states that "where Phil. 1:1 mentions bishops and deacons . . . one suspects that here the editor has updated the greeting to include church officials; apart from this reference, there is no indication that such offices existed during Paul's own time."[5]

It is generally accepted that episcopacy, when it did come into the early Church, was confined to the single congregation, and that often there was more than one Overseer or Bishop per congregation. The change to oversight of several congregations — a district superintendency, if you will — took several centuries.

A clue to the fact that the ascendancy of the bishops was not achieved without resistance is found in the *Didache* (probably A.D. 120-180). After several chapters on discerning the authenticity of prophets and the reception and hospitality to be accorded them, Chapter 15 advises: "Elect, therefore, for yourselves bishops and deacons . . . for they also serve you in the ministry of the prophets and teachers. Do not, therefore, despise them, for they are the honored men among you, along with the prophets and teachers."[6] Episcopacy ultimately triumphed and went on to be monarchicalized, diocesanized, and in Anglican usage, historicized and absolutized. Meanwhile the office of prophet disappeared forever from the Christian Church.

Another clue to the prophetic and charismatic nature of early Church ministry is the fact that during the Montanist controversy (late second, early third century) the orthodox criticized the Montanists because "their ministers were paid." The author adds, with a touch of irony, "It was not long before all Christian ministers were paid."[7]

As for the notion of "clergy," Ernst Käsemann has made it clear that the peculiar distinction between "prophet" and "righteous men" in Matthew (especially Mat. 13:16 ff) is a relic of an earlier Church order. He stresses that the two terms "must not on any account be regarded as . . . [a] distinction between clerics and laymen."[8]

Even the origin of the word *clergy* is obscure. A British Catholic dictionary[9] states: "The word is of course derived from the Greek *kleros,* a 'lot,' a word which frequently occurs in its literal sense in the Septuagint and the New Testament. But how did the word 'lot' come to denote 'the clergy'? The answer to this question is very far from easy." The writer makes a hypothetical reconstruction in which "lot" became "an office allotted," and then "those who held the office." It should not be overlooked, however, that "casting lots," usually portrayed as rolling dice, was not only the method used to claim Christ's garment at the foot of the cross, but also according to Luke, the method of adding Matthias to the Eleven (Acts 1:26). In fact five of the thirteen New Testament uses of *kleros* pertain to decisions, and only one, 1 Peter 5:3, offers any real ground for the development that eventually gave us "clergy."

While the author of the dictionary article just referred to sees the process of changing the referent from "lot" to "office allotted" and then the officeholder completed by the end of the second century, others place it later. A more recent work by another Catholic[10] says that it was only "from the 5th C. on" that *kleros* "was applied in a special way to all who were consecrated to the sacred ministry by either major or minor orders."

It is not necessary to renew the tedious disputes of Protestants and Orthodox with Catholics over the papacy. Nor is it necessary to review the history of the growth in papal authority. The history of the Cardinalate, however, is not as well known. While the ante-Nicene ecclesiastical writers use the words *cardinalis, cardinare, incardinare,* they have no reference to a precise office and the words do not occur in Scripture. The etymological root is *cardo,* meaning "hinge." In the ante-Nicene literature the words are applied to people who were so pivotal that they were like the hinges on which a door swings. However, it was not until Pope Marcellus (304) that the term "cardinal priests" was used to designate those assigned permanently to a fixed parish, as opposed to those "whose connection with a church was loose or temporary."

In Rome itself "cardinal deacons" evolved with charge of the charitable institutions and their chapels located in several sections of the city. The first clear evidence for a "cardinal bishop" comes from the writings of St. Peter Damian (d.1071).[11] In spite of the title "cardinal bishops," lay cardinals were possible until the 1918 Code of Canon Law limited the College of Cardinals to priests. Pope John XXIII further restricted eligibility for that office by decreeing in 1971 that cardinals must come from the ranks of bishops.

This progressive narrowing of eligibility for the cardinalate was analogous to that which accompanied the development of the office of bishop. Some of the best-known figures in the early Church were elected bishop by popular acclamation. In the third century Cyprian says that bishops were chosen "by the suffrage of the clergy and the people" of the province.[12] In some cases the people's choice extended to those who hadn't even been ordained. St. Ambrose was only an unbaptized catechumen when the laity insisted that he be made Bishop of Milan. After accepting with some hesitation, he was then baptized and ordained. St. Gregory of Nazianzus was ordained a priest against his will and under pressure c. 362. He was consecrated a bishop c. 372. Popular election of bishops continued, at least in form, in the Latin Church until the eleventh century.[13]

Returning to Robert Barclay, "We do not believe that there should be any precedence . . . . However, we do believe that some have a more particular call to the work of the ministry" even though anyone has "the liberty to speak or prophesy when moved by the Spirit." [214] "The several measures of grace that are received . . . furnish the basis for the various offices . . . in the Body of Christ which is the Church." [240]

A Functional Ministry

In "the way in which Christians are related to each other," [240] the "ministers we plead for are holy and humble and do not contend for precedence and priority. Instead, they give precedence to others and to serving one another in love" and they "do not desire to be distinguished from others by their garment." [235] As one of the New Testament letters states: "All of you should wrap yourselves in the garment of humility towards each other, because God sets his face against the arrogant, but favours the humble." (1 Pet. 5:5 NEB) *[215]*

The "diversity of names" in the New Testament is given "not to distinguish separate offices, but to denote the various and different ways in which the Spirit functions." They may coincide in the same person. *[211, 213]* Prophecy, for example, "in the sense of foretelling things to come is indeed a distinct gift but not a distinct office." Even our opponents "do not give it a place among their several orders." *[211]*

"Prophecy in the other sense — that is, speaking from the Spirit of Truth — is not only the particular responsibility of pastors and teachers, it is also a common privilege of all believers." *[212]* "Whoever preaches the Gospel" is an evangelist, "consequently every true minister is one," and an apostle is "'one who is sent.' To the extent that every true minister is sent by God, it can also be said that he is an apostle," although those "sent by Christ can be called Apostles *'per eminentiam.'*" *[213]*

As has already been said: "Some have a more particular call to the work of the ministry and . . . are especially equipped for that work by the Lord. We affirm that that work is to instruct, exhort, admonish, oversee and watch over their brethren more frequently and more particularly than the others." There are also elders, who although not "moved to frequent testimony by declaration in words . . . are mature in the experience of the blessed work of Truth in their hearts. Their work is to watch over and privately admonish the young, and to take care of widows, the poor, and the fatherless; and to see that they lack nothing. They see to it that peace, love, unity, harmony, and sound doctrine are preserved in the Church of Christ. This also applies to the deacons mentioned in Acts 6." *[215-216]*

Basically "what we are opposed to is the distinction between clergy and laity, which allows only those who have been educated at schools for that purpose to be admitted to the ministry. This distinction is not found in the Scripture. By it, preaching becomes an art and a trade," and to enter the ministry, one "must also have a Master of Arts degree. This manner of separating men for the ministry was not the practice of the Church in the Apostles' days." *[216]*

In time "reverence" was "annexed to the mere name" of clergyman. As for bishops, "in a short while the succession, instead of being to the nature, virtue, and life of the Apostles, was merely one of name and title . . . a shadow and an empty image. Even this . . . became so metamorphosed" that it could be "asked of the Christian Church . . . whether it was the original structure" at all. *[217]* By further changes it acquired "a secular ministry made up of earthly men who have no Life, Power, or Virtue" and are not "called and sent by God." *[225]* For this state of affairs, the New Testament provides pertinent advice: "You, man of God, must shun all this, and pursue justice, piety, fidelity, love, fortitude, and gentleness." (1 Tim. 6:11 NEB) *[224]*

The Essence of Christian Relationships

If you ask what is necessary "for the transmission and maintenance of a holy fellowship" between Christ "and his people?" *[243]* we answer that it is "communion with Christ" that is "our greatest duty." *[338]* "It is in this inward participation" in the Body of our Lord "by which man is united to God and has fellowship and communion with him" *[332]* that an adequate basis for transmission and maintenance is to be found.

We do not "celebrate" (a word not found in Barclay) what Christ did for us. But we do "participate" in the grace and forgiveness and enablement that Christ earned for us by His obedience, even to death upon a cross. It is a "uniting and mutual participation not of the flesh but of the Spirit." When a soul "tastes and partakes of this heavenly bread, it receives Life again and revives." *[330]*

"Every member has his own particular place in the Body of Christ as Paul so clearly shows in 1 Cor. 12." *[52]* "The gifts we possess differ as they are allotted to us by God's grace." (Rom. 12:6-8 NEB) *[53]* Jesus Christ "promised that he would always be with his children, that he would lead them into all truth, that he would guard them against the devices of the enemy, and that he would establish their faith on an immovable rock" and "he gave them his Spirit as their principal guide." *[56]*

Being nourished by this inward Guide and turning away from unrighteousness "is the bond by which we become 'one spirit with him' (1 Cor. 6:17 Cath-CCD) and so with one another." *[255]* "The Lord has known of our sufferings and reproaches for his testimony's sake. He has caused his power and glory to be all the more abundant among us. He has greatly refreshed us by filling our souls with the sense of his love." *[271]*

George Fox on Order

In comparing Robert Barclay's view of Order with that spelled out by Fox, several things stand out immediately. Where Barclay's emphasis is upon the Spirit as Orderer, Fox's is unmistakably upon Christ. However, since Barclay virtually identifies the living Christ with the Holy Spirit, they are not as far apart as they seem to be at first glance.

For some reason Barclay never uses the term "Gospel Order," which is so frequent in Fox. This is particularly unusual because in most matters he almost always uses Fox's phrasing at least once to identify what it is that he is developing. Thus, for example, while Fox constantly reiterates the phrase "everlasting Gospel," Barclay uses the two words together only enough to indicate that it is not some other gospel that he is talking about. Again, while the "voice" and "prophet" imagery are not as common in Barclay as in Fox, they are there. But in spite of this characteristic habit of at least alluding to Fox's way of handling the same area of doctrine, so far I have not found the phrase "Gospel Order" in Barclay's writings.

Equally peculiarly, Fox in his turn seems to have made little use if any of the Apostle Paul's charisms or "gifts" so prominent in the version of Church Order found in Paul's Epistles. Fox seems to posit a more fluid or more nebulous set of functions, which Christ is at liberty to ordain at whim. Fox makes it quite clear that the origin of all "offices" – or better, "functions" – in the Church is heavenly and spiritual; and he is not too precise on the details of how Christ establishes these in His Church, or which ones are given "permanence" in any sense of that word.

Where Barclay has been seen as the root of a number of problems that emerged later in Quaker history, perhaps Fox is open to the charge that his view of ministry could easily become distorted. In the twentieth century unprogrammed meetings, a good share of the deterioration in the quality of both vocal ministry and pastoral care may be due to this. Fox seems to give authorization for the view that the Call to ministry is evanescent, if not altogether transient. The Call would seem to be no more than an authorization to speak at a given moment, or a summons to fulfill a particular concern of relatively short duration.

Arthur Roberts has pointed out that however transient a ministry based on the gifts of the Spirit might seem in his theology, Fox's setting up of the Second-Day Morning's Meetings indicated an ongoing practical commitment to an itinerant ministry on the part of that meeting's constituents. They met together to coordinate visits to particular churches so they would not all arrive on the same day.

Continuity of the faith was also perpetuated by repetitive practice in a traditional way on the part of the group, aside from any continuing functional commitment to the ministry.

For many generations traditional practices preserved a great deal of the Quaker way of doing things, and in some mysterious fashion seem to have even transmitted some of the Spirit in which they were done. Yet as Lewis Benson points out,[14] the traditional structures now are being dismantled at an alarming rate, and largely on sociological rather than theological grounds, and "without reference to a dynamic principle of regulation."[15]

On a more positive note, as we examine Fox's "Gospel Order," test it in your mind for authenticity and faithfulness to the tenor of Scripture. Were his views more nearly apostolic in *the qualitative sense* and less distorted than the highly institutionalized views of mainstream Christianity? Have they the potential for becoming once again the focus for a genuinely living witness?

Fox's Criteria for Authentic Order

As distinct from "Holy Orders," Fox outlines a *holy* Order[16] that is "not from/of or by man," a statement that recurs with minor variations almost as often as he takes up the nature of Order. What appears at first glance to be an extravagant claim becomes clearer in thrust and scriptural in tone when it is realized that it is a close paraphrase of the Apostle Paul's claims in Gal. 1:1, 11, 12.[17] In the *Jerusalem Bible* version, Paul states that he is "an apostle who does not owe his authority to men or his appointment to any human being but who has been appointed by Jesus Christ and by God . . . ." In the later verses he continues: "I want you to realize this, the Good News I preached is not a human message that I was given by men, it is something I learned only through a revelation of Jesus Christ."

On the other hand Richard Baxter defended Anglican ordination by saying, "They have the people's consent, and the magistrate's allowance, therefore that is true ordination." Fox responded, so did Balaam. So did the chief priests who turned against Christ. But "the ordination of the apostles . . . was not from man nor by man . . . . There is not one of you all that ever durst say ye have heard God's voice immediately from heaven, or Christ's voice, or have the same Spirit the prophets, and apostles, and Christ had."[18] The stress is, in a modern equivalent phrasing, upon "the internal impetus toward fulfillment and wholeness" rather than any "external manifestations" or sources.[19]

Gospel Order is an inclusive order in which the believers constitute the Church, which is established in the same "Light,

Power, and Spirit of Christ by which we are gathered . . . he being in the midst" of His people. "Every believer in the Light . . . is a member of Christ's Church," and an heir "of his Order and of his Government" (Jas. 2:5), "of the increase of which there is no end." (Isa. 9:7) "All who come to God, who is a God of Order, must come by the Grace, Truth, Light, Power, Gospel, Faith, and Anointing – the Word of Life within; and such come to love the Lord Jesus Christ, and to delight in" God and Christ's Kingdom. They "live in the Order of the Gospel," for those who "obey the Voice . . . of Christ Jesus . . . know the Order of Christ."[20]

Christ's Order is a "holy Order of Love and Peace,"[21] "appointed by God"[22] to govern "the assemblies of the righteous."[23] This is the Order of "Jesus Christ and his Gospel."[24] In this Order no earthly person is glorified or exalted "but God and Christ alone. . . . Keep in the Order of this Gospel; and so have Power to admonish, exhort, reprove, and rebuke with all Authority such as talk of Christ, and do not walk in him; such as profess him, and do not possess him."[25]

"In the Lord's everlasting Power," in which is freedom from evil and domination over darkness, "the Lord God Almighty [will] keep you." In the "Gospel, the power of God [Rom. 1:16], in which life and immortality are brought to Light," you may keep and feel your everlasting fellowship and Order."[26] Unlike those Christians who are situated "in the world's invented seats of religion" we are situated in Christ as "in the Apostles' days." For such Christians "Christ was and is their treasure of Wisdom, Life, Knowledge and Salvation . . . . All people now are to hear Christ the Prophet [like Moses, Acts 3:23, 7:37, Deut. 18:18, 19] in this his Gospel of the New Covenant." And "all whom Christ quickens and makes alive, he makes to sit together in the heavenly places." [Eph. 2:6][27]

A group of Puritan ministers at Newcastle maintained that ever since the time of the apostles the call to the ministry has been a mediated call, and officers and elders must be ordained by the mediation of the Church. Fox replied: "All elders and officers of the Church . . . are made immediately by the Spirit." It is "the Power of God [that] Rules and Orders people."[28] Communication with the Spirit of Christ does not give rise to confusion – that occurs only when people "go into disobedience from God . . . [and] are gone from his Image." It is that "in which his holy Order is . . . Truth hath an Order for all things that God did make by Jesus Christ." God's people are "made free indeed by the Truth . . . For Christ bears up his Government . . . He Orders it and establishes it." [Heb. 8:6]

"This is a Day of possessing of Christ, and his Government, and of the Gospel Order . . . do not lose" your Order, even "though some may slight it. For the foundation of our men's and women's meetings is Christ Jesus" who surpasses "all false orders and foundations."[29] "The gathering is to Christ,"[30] "the Spiritual Man," who is "the Author and Finisher" of this "Spiritual Order."[31] It was not created by the "author of strife,"[32] for the "serpent is against" it.[33]

In this "holy and heavenly Order"[34] "males and females are all one in Christ Jesus." [Gal. 3:28][35] "This is the Day for all to take their possessions of this Gospel Order, which was the Apostles' . . . Keep this comely Order." [1 Cor. 7:35 Jer B][36] "See that Virtue flow[s], and see that all your words be gracious, and see that Love flows, which bears all things." See "that kindness, tenderness, and gentleness may be among you, and that the fruits of the good Spirit may abound": and that "in all things . . . God may be glorified, exalted, and honored."[37]

Testify "against all that which is contrary to Jesus, the Heavenly Man . . . and see that everyone's affections be set on things above."[38] It is the "duty of all Christians to walk in Christ." [Ps. 1] All whose conversation [i.e., "deportment"] is Ordered aright[39] lack nothing, "being Ordered by the holy, pure, peaceable, and gentle Wisdom of God." And dwelling in this, "nothing can get between you and the Lord God."[40] This "good Order"[41] is a "glorious Order"[42] and a "joyful Order" which "keeps all hearts Pure, . . . in everlasting Peace, Unity, and Order."[43]

By this Order "act for God" and in it "do business and service for him in his Church,"[44] "serving one another in the Love and Wisdom of God"[45]; "looking after the poor, taking care for orderly proceedings in marriages and other matters relating to the Church of Christ."[46]

"We are not our own, and are not to live to ourselves, not to order ourselves, but to live unto him and be Ordered, Ruled, and Governed by him . . . to be Counselled by him, and Led by him, and Taught by him, as he is our Heavenly Prophet, and to be fed by him our Heavenly Shepherd, in his heavenly pasture and fold; and to be Overseen by him, as he is our Heavenly Bishop."[47]

"The fellowship in the Gospel . . . is a perfect one,"[48] and this fellowship is not found "in the form without the Power."[49] There is "no true fellowship but in the Pure Faith, Light, Spirit and Gospel of God and Christ."[50] "Walk in the Gospel, the Power of

God, which is the Authority of your meetings."[51] "Keep in the Power. . . . If ye lose it, . . . ye will not soon regain it."[52] "In this Day of his New Covenant, and New Testament . . . God poureth forth of his Spirit upon all flesh [Acts 2:17-21, Joel 2:28-32], which none are to grieve, vex, nor quench, nor rebel against but obey it." [Eph. 4:30; 1 Thes. 5:19; 1 Pet. 4:17][53]

Summary

The uniqueness of Gospel Order consists in *the quality of the relationships and proceedings.* It is not inherent in the way in which they are structured. Gospel Order derives from a preclerical apostolic situation in which there was no dichotomy between classes of persons. Nor were there any graded states of increasing authority for either persons or groups. The same people could be organized in various ways for different purposes. Since loyalty was always to a common Lord, there was no need to interlock or subordinate groupings that corresponded to geographical areas, or others that served particular purposes. Faithfulness and obedience, *not sacralized authoritarian structures,* were the opposite of confusion.

The authority in Gospel Order derives solely from this faithfulness to *Christ's values and demands.* The way in which the individual discerns these is measured and tested against that of the group's as a whole. The group frequently offers assistance and such advice as is consistent with the commonly understood values and demands of the heavenly Shepherd, Bishop, and Guide, who makes his will known without mediation.

Although under Gospel Order appointments are made for correlation and administration, they carry no arbitrary authority although responsibility is clearly delimited as to scope or geography. The primary qualifications for appointment emphasize concerned experience and spiritual sensitivity.

A clerk, for example, "presides" only to the extent of organizing the proceedings into a proposed agenda. When the agenda has been accepted as proposed or amended, the clerk's role becomes essentially facilitative: requesting adherence to the agenda, keeping discussion within limits that will equalize the opportunity for all to participate, calling attention to points that are being overlooked, or perhaps proposing that the group may be ready to proceed to the next matter. If the clerk wishes to contribute ideas to the discussion, he/she requires permission to step out of the role of clerk temporarily.

The conducting of a meeting for business according to the principles of Gospel Order involves an intricate interplay of insights and counsel, and a balancing of traditional procedures and interests with an openness to new ways and concerns. The method employs not only gifts of information but gifts of evaluation and synthesis. And the intellectual approach is always subordinated to the spiritual and the revelational.

Everything is done under a sense of Presence. All seek to be obedient to Christ's will in both the details of the undertaking and the way in which they are done. At a point in the proceedings, which will vary in each instance and for each matter under discussion, the clerk's most important role comes into play. She/he then attempts to express the "sense of the meeting" by framing a minute. When done properly this recognizes where various comments have been supplemental or in harmony in spite of apparent divergences. The proposed minute may be accepted as written or it may be amended from the floor. Perhaps it is unacceptable and indicates the need for further discussion and clarification because the basis for agreement is still inadequate.

Legislation subject to such conditions seeks neither power nor advantage. Groups of like opinion do not become factions but, instead, they seek reconciliation with those of a different mind. There is no attempt to persuade unduly. And, while no value is placed on artfully phrased rhetoric, precision and clarity of speech are highly valued.

The touchstone for all that takes place and what gives Authority to the proceedings is conformity to the Truth of Christ and to His will. When serious matters are being discussed, the tone of the discussion should be prayerful, yet seasoned with a distinctive type of humor that puts things in perspective without wounding or offending. In every detail of methods and goals, faithfulness is required to the Gospel that Jesus preached, the life He lived, and the self-effacement and suffering He endured in order to make possible the redemption of humankind and the cosmos.

Notes to Chapter 6

Italic figures in brackets within the text refer to page numbers in *Barclay's Apology in Modern English*.

1. Heinrich Denzinger, *Enchiridion Symbolorum Definitionum et Declarationum de Rebus Fidei et Morum* (1923 ed.): 1313, 1609. Also Code of Canon Law (1917) C. 732.1.
2. William E. Addis and Thomas Arnold, *A Catholic Dictionary*, 15th ed., rev. by T. B. Scannell (London: Virtue, 1975) s.v. "Order, Holy."

3 *The Fourth World Conference on Faith and Order, Montreal 1963*, ed. by P. C. Rodger and Lukas Vischer (New York: Association Press, 1964), Report of Section 1, paragraph 21, page 45.
4 It is true that the *taxis* found there can mean (1) A "fixed succession or order," and it is used in that sense in Luke 1:8. However, there it means no more than that Zechariah was *taking his turn* in rotating assignment of the Temple duties. (2) It can mean "[good] order," as in 1 Cor. 14:40, where it is coupled with *euschemenos*. The various versions vary considerably in their rendering of that passage, but none gives the weight of legalism or arbitrary authority to it. It signifies no more than done in an "orderly manner" (Weymouth) or "orderly way" (Goodspeed) or done "decently" (NEB), or done "properly and in an orderly manner" (NAB), or "with propriety and in order" (JerB), or "honestly and in order." (Tyndale)

In the other New Testament passage employing sense (2), the Colossians are commended (Col. 2:5) for their "good discipline" (Weymouth), "getting along so well" (LB), their "harmony" (Goodspeed, JerB), their orderliness ("orderly" TEV, "orderly array" NEB), and solidity (i.e., "solid steadfastness" and "orderly way" Philips), the "resolute firmness" with which they "stand together." (TEV) The coupled term *stereoma* has obviously influenced some of these translations.

Taxis can mean (3) a "position, post." And this would seem to be more favorable to institutional or juridical interpretation, except for the fact that it does not appear anywhere in the New Testament.

Finally, it can mean (4) "nature, quality, manner, condition, appearance." There are a number of occurrences in Hebrews where this sense applies (Heb. 5:6, 10; 6:20; 7:11, 17, 21). There they signify that Jesus was a high priest "according to the nature of" or "just like" Melchizedek. In these passages it does connote "higher rank" as well as an "entirely different nature," but extending them to His Church. This analysis of the four meanings of *taxis* is based on Bauer-Arndt-Gingrich, *A Greek-English Lexicon of the New Testament and Other Early Christian Literature*, 4th ed. (Cambridge: University Press, 1952).
5 Leander E. Keck, *Paul and His Letters*, in the Proclamation Commentaries series ed. by Gerhard Krodel (Philadelphia: Fortress Press, 1979), p. 13.
6 *The Apostolic Fathers;* transl. by F. X. Glimm; J.M.F.Marique, S.J.; G.G. Walsh, S.J.; in The Fathers of the Church: A New Translation; series editorial director Ludwig Schopp, vol. 1 (Washington: Catholic University Press, 1962), p. 183.
7 Marjorie Strachey, *The Fathers Without Theology* (New York: Braziller, 1958), p. 172.
8 Ernst Käsemann, "The Beginnings of Christian Theology," in *Journal for Theology and the Church*, ed. by Robert W. Funk, vol. 6 (New York: Herder & Herder, 1969), p. 28.

The reorientation of Roman Catholic thought on the set-apart ministry in recent years has been remarkable. As recently as 1939 Stanislaus Woywod, O.F.M. stated in his *A Practical Commentary on the Code of Canon Law* (New York: Wagner) vol. 1, p. 485, that Canon 948 "repeats a fundamental principle of Catholic faith, namely, that the distinction between the clergy and the laity is of divine origin."

However, Edward Schillebeeckx, O.P. states in a recent book whose very title is significant, *Ministry: Leadership in the Community of Jesus Christ*(New York: Crossroad, 1981), p. 5: "Apart from apostleship or the 'apostolate,' the [first] Christian communities did not receive any kind of church order from the hands of Jesus when he still shared our earthly history .... This primary, fundamental datum of the New Testament must already make us very cautious: we must not be led astray into speaking too casually about divine ordinances and particular dispositions in respect of the community and its leaders or ministry."
9 Addis and Arnold, *op. cit.,* pp. 189-190.

10 Louis Bouyer, Cong. Or., *Dictionary of Theology* (New York: Desclee, 1955), p. 89, s.v. "cleric, clergy."
11 Addis and Arnold, *op. cit.*, p. 114, s.v. "cardinal."
12 *Ep. 68*, ed. by Hartel, 745.
13 Addis and Arnold, *op. cit.*, s.v. "bishop."
14 Lewis Benson, "The People of God and Gospel Order," in *The Church in Quaker Thought and Practice,* ed. by Charles F. Thomas (Philadelphia: Faith and Life Movement, 1979), distributed by Friends World Committee, Section of the Americas, pp. 16-26.
15 Benson, *loc. cit.*, p. 17.
16 Holiness as a godlike quality cannot be overemphasized: "God's goodness is holy. His Being is holy. His anger is holy. His Love is holy. Holiness therefore points to the unconditioned, the transcendent element of deity . . . ." – Langdon Gilkey, *Maker of Heaven and Earth: The Christian Doctrine of Creation* (Garden City, N.Y.: Doubleday Anchor, 1959), p. 98.
17 The obscurity of the KJV's "not of men, neither by men" (v. 1) and "not after man," neither "of men" (vv. 11, 12) becomes particularly lucid in the *Jerusalem Bible*, which has translated them into the clearest modern English of any translation I have seen.
18 George Fox, *Works of George Fox,* 8 vols. (Philadelphia: M.T.C. Gould, 1831) 3:113-114.
19 The phrasing is from a chapter on "World Order and Authentic Religion," from Gerald and Patricia Mische, *Toward a Human World Order: Beyond the National Security Straitjacket* (Ramsey, N.J.: Paulist Press, 1977) p. 331.
20 Fox, *Works of George Fox,* 8:174, 183, 184.
21 George Fox, *Journal,* Bi-Centenary edition (London, 1891), II:244.
22 Isaac Penington, *Works,* London: Samuel Clark, 1761 I:617-619.
23 Fox, *Works of George Fox,* 7:250.
24 *Ibid.,* 8:82.
25 *Ibid.,* 8:78, 79.
26 *Ibid.,* 8:90.
27 Fox, *Journal,* Bi-Centenary edition, II:364.
28 Fox, *Works of George Fox,* 3:146.
29 *Ibid.,* 6:182-183, 184. 8:46.
30 *Ibid.,* 7:286.
31 *Ibid.,* 8:189.
32 *Ibid.,* 8:90.
33 *Ibid.,* 8:71.
34 *Ibid.,* 8:67.
35 *Ibid.,* 8:190.
36 *Ibid.,* 8:51.
37 *Ibid.,* 8:33.
38 *Ibid.,* 8:33-34.
39 *Ibid.,* 8:71.
40 *Ibid.,* 8:148.
41 George Fox, *Journal,* revised edition by John L. Nickalls (Cambridge: University Press, 1952), p. 515.
42 *Ibid.,* 525.
43 Fox, *Journal,* Bi-Centenary edition, II:244.
44 *Ibid.,* II:247.
45 Fox, *Works of George Fox,* 7:85.
46 Fox, *Journal,* Bi-Centenary edition, II:247.
47 Fox, *Works of George Fox,* 5:203.
48 *Ibid.,* 7:243.
49 *Ibid.,* 5:105.
50 *Ibid.,* 7:244.
51 Fox, *Journal,* Bi-Centenary edition, II:244.
52 *Ibid.,* II:250.
53 Fox, *Works of George Fox,* 8:171-172.

Chapter 7
SCRIPTURE

One of the stickier wickets for the theologians under scrutiny was the place of Scripture. Barclay did an even better job of opening the door to misconceptions and a general muddying of the waters on the subject of Scripture than he did in introducing Luther's "visibility" and "invisibility" into his discussions of the Church. By using the traditional framework of Sources of Revelation and Authority to discuss Scripture's role he automatically "bought into" a hierarchical ranking of Sources and a graduated series of roles.

In so doing he arrived at a view of Scripture as subordinate and secondary to the Holy Spirit in Authority. But it is not enough to label his view as erroneous or simply dismiss it as inadequate. Not only did the negative terminology obscure what he was trying to say, but it made it difficult to realize that actually what he was trying to enunciate was a method for interpreting the Bible – something that today would be called "hermeneutics."

So new was the territory Barclay and the others were exploring that the Latin word *hermeneutica*, which preceded the English term "hermeneutics," was just being introduced into theological discussions in Germany. After Barclay's writing of the *Apology*, 60 years would elapse before the word "hermeneutics" would appear in English (1737, according to the *Oxford English Dictionary*). Johann Conrad Dannhauer (1603-1666) is generally credited with originating the concept behind the word. However, Johann Gerhard (1582-1637) and his pupil Salomon Glass (1593-1656) preceded Dannhauer in developing the subject matter that came to be included in the discussion of hermeneutical principles.[1] "Hermeneutics" embraces the whole range of interpretation from exegesis (the literal meaning of a particular text) to restating the truth of a group of texts, indeed whole areas of Scripture, in terms that are more in accord with modern thought patterns.

Barclay's characterization of the Scriptures "as a secondary rule that is subordinate to the Spirit" [46] has never been a satisfactory statement. Friends themselves sometimes relegated Scripture to an inconsequential role partly because of it, and others were ready to class Quakers as unchristian in the light of it.

Yet when one takes into account everything the early Friends had to say about Scripture and looks at the way in which they used it, they were far from downgrading the Bible. Not only were they "willing for all of our own doctrines and practices to be tried by" the Scriptures and added that any doctrine "contrary to their testimony may properly be rejected as false," [60] they considered "the Scriptures undoubtedly and unequivocally the finest writings in the world." [46]

What did they say that was really new and constructive in their approach, at least as far as the English religious scene was concerned?

(1) The Bible was not a mine for the excavation of "proof texts." Many of their contemporaries were quite willing to take any scriptural statement out of context, or completely detach it from its intent if the words themselves (or even part of them) seemed to support a particular doctrine. It is an approach that is still around.[2]

(2) Scripture was not to be subservient to philosophy. The intellectual "notions" of that discipline (particularly as represented by Scholasticism) were not to be imposed upon biblical texts to make them say what one would like them to say. While these were not the first theologians to reject Scholastic philosophy – the Lutherans had done it, only to have their own Protestant Neo-Scholasticism follow, which developed even finer distinctions and shadings of thought – the group we are considering understood the consequences of imposing philosophical distinctions on Scripture as leading "into such a labyrinth of contention that it is far more likely to make a skeptic than a Christian." [200]

(3) The "outer meaning" or superficial sense of the words was de-emphasized in favor of the "deeper meanings."

Nevertheless, in looking at a text in relation to doctrine, it was the "plain meaning" that should be sought. In "open places," Samuel Fisher said, "leave it as it is" (p. 428); the texts should be taken "as the words import." (p. 657) Someone, perhaps Vernard Eller, gave an updated version of this idea when he put it (roughly, from memory): "If the plain sense makes good sense, don't look for another sense." This "plain sense" did not exclude metaphor or spiritual interpretations, but it did exclude far-fetched exegesis. Integrity was valued more highly than ingenuity.

(4) Christ was the guide through His Spirit in arriving at the "deeper meaning" of a text that had both superficial and basic overtones. This applied not only to the illumination of grace but also to the consistency of the particular text with the basic teachings and ministry of the earthly Jesus.

(5) All of the Bible – "the whole scope" (S.F., p. 623) – should be taken into account; and all statements on any one subject should be reconciled on the basis of "common sense" rather than any elaborate or roundabout rules of "logic." Circumstances, historical epochs, the character of the speaker, all played a part, with the specifics of actual application left to the illumination of the Spirit of Christ.

(6) Historic and linguistic clues, grammar, and consistency with the major themes of the Bible as well as distinguishing whether individual statements were didactic, experiential, legal, or narrative in character, should all enter into the process of interpretation.

(7) Perhaps the most significant insight of our authors was their realization of the experiential dimension of the Bible. Not only were the Scriptures "holy writings which possess more than earthly beauty," but their use "imparts strength and hope." [50] Their major effect in the final analysis is redemptive, especially where there is resonance between ancient problems and failures and those that plague later readers. The accounts of God's help in such situations give evidence that God cares and has compassion on the children of His creation.

(8) In preparation for the discernment of the correct interpretation of a particular text by the guidance of the Spirit of Christ, variant readings of the text of the Bible and various versions (or translations) should be consulted, as well as the commentaries.

(Note: An addendum following the Notes at the end of this chapter illustrates these principles with quotations.)

Experiential or Revelational Preeminence As Espoused by Fox

While all of the authors dealt with in this volume used Scripture in the constructive ways that have been outlined, none equaled George Fox for the tremendous insights that must have been "revelations" (Fox himself would have called them "openings") by his heavenly Lord. Much of what he saw with lucidity is now being discovered by the tortuous and tedious methods of biblical scholarship. But often the results of such study, even though the work may extend over a century or more, are meager, partial, and tentative; whereas Fox's conclusions tended to be far-reaching reorientations of major aspects of faith.

Unfortunately for the researcher, Fox's use of Scripture is extremely complex, and his method can only be discovered with great labor and a good deal of eyestrain. In trying to determine what he has to say and how he arrives at it, one needs first to search concordances by the hour to discover what passages he is referring to and whether he is quoting, paraphrasing, or simply reminiscing. Although he usually quotes the KJV, the exceptions often prove illuminating and demonstrate his familiarity with other versions. After the biblical allusions or quotations have been identified, long careful meditation and analysis are required to discover which are the key or palmary texts and how they relate to each other.

A further complication is added by the fact that in proclamation Fox often used a kind of biblical shorthand. Phrases – often no more than paired words like "everlasting Gospel," for example – are expected to have a mnemonic effect, and not only to bring to mind the full text but to bring a whole range of associations into the consciousness of his hearers.

A final complication is that Fox insisted that only Scripture terms should be used in theology. The constructive aspect of this is that we are kept closer to the personal, relational, and experiential patterns so characteristic of Hebrew thought. But a number of difficulties arise from this restriction when one is in unexplored territory. And often, lacking a clue as to what the relationships are between the texts that are being evoked by a whole barrage of them strung together, one is apt to feel more besieged than consoled.

Thanks to the Herculean efforts of Lewis Benson over a period of many years in employing a phenomenological approach, at least a dozen of the major themes as well as many minor ones have been identified. And thanks to his generosity in making his Rolodex notes available, others can build on the solid foundations that he has laid.

Fox's insights did not stop with identifying the plain meaning or even the spiritual significance of particular passages. He not only recovered the early Christian understanding of the Church and its mission and ministry, but above all he developed a fresh and more comprehensive view of the functions of its living Lord. Christ was truly the Alpha and Omega for Fox—being both *the meaning* and *the method* of interpreting the Christian faith.[3] Christ was the inaugurator of the End Time, the partial realization of the Kingdom, and both the termination and the replacement (the end in both senses) of all sacrifices, ceremonies, laws, commandments—for He Himself was their living embodiment. He was the fulfillment of messianic, prophetic, and apocalyptic expectations. The result of this living lordship was the replacement of a system of rites and rules by an ever-present guide who provided new understandings, new roles, and new power for His disciples.

The Role of Scripture

Where is Christ to be found? "Some consider Christ to be present in one way, some in another. Some look for Him in the Scriptures, or books . . . . Some take refuge in an external barren faith, and they think that all will be well if they merely believe firmly enough that he died for their past and future sins." Yet they overlook "the appearance of Christ in their hearts" and "many consider us fools and madmen," because "we invite them to mind the Light in themselves, and we request them to believe in Christ as he exists in them." *[111]*

Many Protestants declare Scripture to be their "only rule," but that does not prevent arguments over its meaning, in which "one pleads for his sense, another for his."[4] The cogent but scattered comments of Samuel Fisher express concisely what the Quakers were objecting to in Puritan views of the Bible. Not only is the Bible "adored and idolized" by the Puritans, he says,[5] but they "dethrone Christ,"[6] and "commit high treason to the supremacy, crown, and dignity of Christ, and his Light and Spirit."[7] One must always bear in mind that Scripture is merely "the words of Christ,"[8] whereas "the only sure foundation of the faith and Church" is "Christ himself, his Light and Spirit."[9] He is "the true living Word."[10]

Furthermore, in spite of Puritan claims, Scripture does not serve as the basis for the entire Puritan faith. For many of their principles they are "forced to recur to Tradition; and can by no means prove [that part of their doctrine] from Scripture." On the other hand, our "principles are found in Scripture, word by word . . . plainly couched in Scripture-words without addition or commentary" and it is not necessary to use any of those "strained and far-fetched consequences which men have invented."[11]

Barclay's close associate and mentor for some of his theology, George Keith, asserted: "We have a two-fold evidence, which no heretic can justly lay claim to. The one is the inward evidence of the Spirit of God . . . . The other is the Testimony of the Scriptures, which I affirm in the name of the people called Quakers, is the best external and outward evidence and rule that can be given."[12] But, Penn stated, "Parrots may learn Scripture, but can never experience it. And those know little better, who know not by experience: they are unprofitable canters indeed, who confidently talk of what they have never felt."[13] Quakers were raised up "for no other purpose than to declare that which our eyes have seen, our ears have heard, and which our hands have handled of the Eternal Word; in opposition to private opinions, conjectures, and interpretations of men" and to reduce people "to faith in and obedience to the universal grace which brings salvation"; which alone "can restore sound judgment concerning God, and effect redemption from iniquity."[14]

In another statement by Barclay and Keith, an interesting interrelationship between Scripture and Spirit is described in rather Scholastic terms: "We know the Scripture's testimony by the Spirit, *tanquam a priori,* as we know the effect by the cause; and we know the Spirit's testimony by the Scriptures, *tanquam a posteriori,* as we know the cause by the effect; and so both are objective." Yet, they are "objective" in different ways. Unfortunately, however, this statement takes us back to "subordination"; for the statement continues: "Because the objective evidence of the Spirit is a self-evidence and primary, the objective evidence of the Scripture is but derived and secondary."[15] Since the Latin phrases mean "as it were, beforehand" and "as it were, subsequently," one could also read the statement as contrasting deductive knowledge with inductive.

Vatican II revealed how difficult it is to develop an adequate doctrine of the Sources of Revelation. Under combined Catholic-revisionist and Protestant criticism, the old doctrine of two independent Sources—Scripture and Tradition—gave way to seeing them together as "a single sacred deposit." (10) In this they are "bound closely together and communicate one with the other" (9) like a mirror. *Dei Verbum,* the Constitution on Revelation, elaborated other contributing factors. The "sayings of the Holy Fathers" (Patristics) received a distinctive role. While they were subordinated to Tradition, they were also linked with the "experience of spiritual realities" and "preaching." Together, these two factors were seen as contributing to "growth in insight." (8)

"Human reason" is mentioned (6) as having a confirmatory role, and "the task of giving an authentic interpretation of the Word of God . . . has been entrusted to the living teaching office of the Church *alone"* [emphasis added]. However, this autonomy is hedged a bit by stating, "yet this magisterium is not superior to the Word of God, but is its servant." It is further limited by the claim that this magisterial or teaching office "teaches only what has been handed on to it," (10) thus providing for continuity.

In a doxological conclusion to the chapter (II) from which all of these statements have been drawn, "the supremely wise arrangement of God" is lauded. In that "arrangement," not only are "Sacred Tradition, Sacred Scripture, and the Magisterium of the Church" so interconnected and so closely associated that one "cannot stand without the others," but each works "in its own way *under* the action of the one Holy Spirit." (10) [emphasis added]

While Barclay's epistemology did not involve as many different elements as Vatican II's did, it might have been better had he limited the Holy Spirit to a similar *supervisory role.* In that way his revelational triad could have avoided any explicit or precise "subordination" of the other two elements – Scripture and inward revelation (or illumination). Although Barclay did not give Patristics a place in his theorizing about revelation, nevertheless the early Church Fathers played an important part in his theology. The so-called *"consensus Patrum,"* whereby the Church Fathers were supposed to have agreed on all important matters, had been challenged already by Jean Daillé (1594-1670). Daillé demonstrated that consensus was an illusion and the Fathers rarely agreed in any number on anything.[16] Barclay was able to follow the rules laid down in Daillé's *The Right Use of the Fathers* in a constructive way that allowed their Testimony to substantiate his theological claims. The quotations he introduces from them are still credible and serviceable.

The flaw in Barclay's principles of interpretation, however, was that accepting the standard framework of Sources of Revelation resulted in placing an intermediary between *the Source* and the believer. This opened the door to all sorts of potential mediations that result in quite different emphases. As soon as mediation enters there is no longer reliance upon a living Lord who will instruct His people *now* in His will for them. It is precisely their fresh and constant return to the Source, Christ Himself, which constitutes the best single reason why Quakers have pioneered in so many areas of Christian social change — elimination of slavery, prison reform, educational reform, and humane treatment of the mentally ill, just to name a few.

While in due time by the less direct methods of magisterial consultation and decision others ultimately develop a theology that permits them to take up the same kind of emphases, they often seem inhibited at the level of initial innovation. Slave-owning was abolished among Quakers (who, originally, were heavy slaveholders themselves) one hundred years before the Civil War decided the issue for other Christians in the United States. Currently the ordination of women is a major issue in many Christian churches, but for over 300 years Friends have given women an equal role in all aspects of the ministry and government of the Church.

No doctrine of the Sources that I am aware of makes adequate use of the role of spiritual experience in hermeneutics (although Vatican II's *Dei Verbum* did give it some mention). Is it enough to claim the Church's guidance by the Spirit when in practice it is unfettered (so to speak) only at great Conciliar gatherings? Barclay's claim of *primacy* for the Spirit at the expense of Scripture was certainly a serious flaw, but to *minimize* and *restrict* the role of the Spirit and religious experience in hermeneutical matters as many Protestant theologies do may be even worse. The Anglican theologian, John Macquarrie, without attempting a magisterial role, has provided a very useful and sophisticated discussion of these various factors, which reveals the complexity of the matter and touches on some of the problems encountered in this kind of approach.[17]

One fact is certain: if the ecumenical movement is ever to develop a truly ecumenical theology, the virtually unmentioned and almost wholly unexamined practice of considering particular centuries normative — the era of Reformation and Counter-reformation, or the era of the first seven Ecumenical Councils, or the high tide of Scholasticism, or whatever — will need to be abandoned. Apostolicity in any genuine first century sense has been largely ignored until now. It will have to come into its own. Just as modern architecture had to arrive at a functionalism by stripping away inherited Classical, Renaissance, Romanesque, Gothic, or other eclectic ornamentation, doctrine will need to be radically reassessed and stripped of many accumulated distortions, overdevelopments, and misunderstandings if any lasting integrity is to develop in ecumenical discussions.

This was the starting point for George Fox in the seventeenth century and one wonders whether the ecumenical movement will ever have the courage to say, as he did, that the Church has gotten so far from its beginning intents and purposes in so many areas that reform is out of the question, and it will be necessary to begin again and build anew. Whether or not that ever happens, it will be interesting to see how well some of the early Quaker insights stand up. Most certainly the view of the role of Scripture and of its interpretation touches on many of the matters that are current problems today.

Notes to Chapter 7

Italic figures in brackets within the text refer to page numbers in *Barclay's Apology in Modern English.*

1. For details see Dean Freiday, *The Bible—Its Criticism, Interpretation and Use—In 16th and 17th century England* (Manasquan, NJ: C & Q S, 1979), pages 65 and 154. This is Catholic and Quaker Studies No. 4 which may be ordered from C & Q S, 1110 Wildwood Ave., Manasquan, NJ 08736.
2. A report presented to the Bristol meeting of the Faith & Order Commission of the World Council of Churches in 1967, entitled "The Significance of the Hermeneutical Problem for the Ecumenical Movement," found in *New Directions in Faith and Order* (Geneva: WCC, 1968), pp. 32-41 and reprinted in *The Bible: Its Authority and Interpretation in the Ecumenical Movement,* ed. by Ellen Flesseman-van Leer, F. & O. Paper No. 99 (Geneva: WCC, 1980), pp. 30-41, says (Bristol, p. 34; F. & O. No. 99, p. 32), "It is dangerous to quote isolated texts as 'proof texts' as has often been done. Small literary units cannot be rightly used without testing and checking their functions as parts of larger complexes. There are, however, certain sentences which, after testing for congruence with the tendency of larger units, prove to be good summaries or epitomes of significant thoughts, and it is then legitimate to cite them as such."
3. Christ is "the Word of God, who fulfilled the words; the Scriptures end in him" (George Fox, *Works of George Fox,* 8 vols., Philadelphia: M.T.C. Gould, 1831, 3:462). At the same time, it is Christ who "opens the Scriptures . . . by the Holy Ghost" (Fox, *Works of George Fox,* 4:406); for "no creature can read the Scriptures to profit thereby, but [those] who come to the Light and Spirit that gave them forth" (Fox, *Works of George Fox,* 7:78). It is by the "Light of Christ and his Spirit by which they might know the Scriptures." (George Fox, *Journal,* revised edition by John L. Nickalls, Cambridge: University Press, 1952, pp. 352ff).
4. Robert Barclay, "Truth Cleared" (1670) in His Collected Works, entitled *Truth Triumphant . . .* (usually cited as *Works*) (London: Northcott, 1692), page 17.
5. Samuel Fisher, *Works* (title actually begins *Rusticus ad Academicos . . .)* (London: Wilson, 1660), page 230.
6. *Ibid.,* p. 248.
7. *Ibid.,* p. 401.
8. *Ibid.,* p. 478.
9. *Ibid.,* p. 14.
10. *Ibid.,* pp. 336 and 443.

11 Barclay *Works,* in the Preface to the "Catechism," p. 112.
12 George Keith (1675) in Robert Barclay *Works,* p. 576.
13 Wm. Penn (1673), *Works,* II:222.
14 Wm. Penn (1668), *Works,* I:130.
15 George Keith "Quakerism Confirmed" (1675) in Robert Barclay *Works,* p. 608.
16 For a brief epitome of Daillé's significance see Dean Freiday *The Bible . . . ,* Note 1 to the Introduction, p. 121.
17 John Macquarrie, *Principles of Christian Theology* (New York: Scribners, 1966), pp. 4-17.

Addendum to Chapter 7

QUOTATIONS TO SUBSTANTIATE THE PRINCIPLES OF INTERPRETATION STATED IN CHAPTER 7

(1) The Bible was not a mine for the excavation of "proof texts":

This is well exemplified by the fact that what was perhaps the central proclamation of the "everlasting Gospel," George Fox's claim that "Christ has come to teach his people himself," is not found in any single text. It represents conflation and epitomization of a whole group of texts. Penn, interestingly, cites these: John 14:26; 16:13. Acts 20:32. 1 Cor. 2:9-12. Titus 2:11-12. 1 John 2:20-21 (Wm. Penn, *Works,* III:249).

A particular text might be broadened in its application either on the basis of common logic or generally accepted maxims. For example, the "yea, yea; or nay, nay" passage (Mt. 5:37) is read not simply as a prohibition of taking oaths in court, but "since truth-speaking takes in and relates to controversies among men, as well as other parts of human converse, this text is a measure of truth-speaking on all those occasions also." (W.P. III:241)

Or a major thrust of the Bible might be sought through analysis of such well-known documents as the Ten Commandments or the Sermon on the Mount. "The Decalogue, or Ten Commandments, were little more than . . . an epitome and transcript of the law writ in man's heart by the finger of God . . . it relates to that righteousness which is indispensable and immutable." (W.P. III:59) "Is it the religion of Christ wherein you walk? Read his holy Sermon on the Mount." (W.P. II:392) "The great intention of this Sermon is to press people to a more excellent righteousness than that of the Scribes and Pharisees." (W.P. III:71)

SCRIPTURE 73

(2) Scripture was not to be subservient to philosophy:

We "refuse any other terms than those the Holy Ghost has given us . . . in the very language of Scripture . . . [to] safely and properly declare our belief." (W.P. III:50) Put aside "all those things called Articles of Faith and Canons of the Church that are not to be found in express terms in Scripture, or so plainly authorized by Scripture" that they "may with ease be discerned by every honest and conscientious person." (W.P. III:57)

"The constructions and conclusions of men from sacred writ, and not the text itself, have been enjoined and imposed as essential to eternal salvation, and external Christian communion." (W.P. III:93) For instance, "where do you find 'plenary satisfaction' in the Bible?" (W.P. III:261)

The Bible is not for stoic philosophers to explain by their "own natural understandings" (Samuel Fisher *Works* 256), nor should we substitute "the unprofitable metaphysics of the heathen." (W.P. II:262) Wm. Penn quoted one of the Labadists, who stated: "Scholars now coming among you, will be apt to mix school-learning amongst your purer and simpler language and thereby obscure the brightness of the testimony." (W.P. II:467) "Opinions are all those propositions or conclusions . . . which either are not expressly laid down in Scripture, or not so evidently deducible from Scripture as to leave no occasion of doubt of the truth of them . . . [and] are either carried so high, spun so fine, or so disguised by barbarous School [i.e., 'Scholastic'] terms, that they are rather a bone of contention, than a bond of concord to religious societies." (W.P. III:46)

In the case of the doctrine of the Trinity, "your proof, 1 Jn. 5:7 . . . will not support your charge, because it contains not . . . [the words] 'three persons . . . .' We believe the Scripture, though we reject that interpretation, and we own three witnesses, and that those three are one; without allowing the intricacy and confusion of the Schools." (W.P. III:260) Christians should only "use the form of sound words given them by the Holy Ghost." (W.P. III:262)

"It is about the meaning of this, and the intention of that place of Scripture the contest hath been and still is . . . . Oh, that we would but be impartial and see our own overplus to the Scriptures and retrench that redundancy." (W.P. III:94)

(3) The "outer meaning" or superficial sense of the words was to be de-emphasized in favor of the deeper meanings:

Because they sought the truth in depth, Friends were charged with "turning the sacred truths of Scripture into jejune allegories." (W.P. III:254) They answered that in interpreting specific texts: "Here they are proper, there metaphorical: in one place literally, in another mystically to be accepted." (W.P. II:6) They cited the fact that in Christ's own declaration, "the word 'body' is figuratively used, as it imports . . . the food of the saints, their spiritual nourishment and subsistence." (W.P. III:255) Penn interpreted Noah's Ark allegorically, as "the most apt and lively emblem of toleration—a kind of natural temple of indulgence. . . . We find two of every living creature dwelling together . . . as well of the unclean as clean kind." (W.P. II:531)

(4) Christ was the guide through His Spirit in arriving at the "deeper meaning" of a text:

We have not "denied or slighted the blessed manifestation of the Son of God in the flesh" but "we should not satisfy ourselves only with what Christ did . . . so long ago . . . we should know and feel him by his Light and Spirit." (W.P. III:256) And, "these holy Scriptures are not to be understood, but by the discoveries, teachings, and operations of that Eternal Spirit from whence they came." (W.P. II:407) "Christ is the only right expounder, as well as the Author of holy Scripture: and without whose Light, Spirit, and Grace they cannot be profitably read." (W.P. III:274) "As face answers face in a glass . . . the Scripture and the Spirit answer each other." (W.P. III:250) Without "Christ, the great and eminent Word, . . . we can never understand nor believe the Scriptures as we should." (W.P. II:210) "The internal testimony of the Spirit . . . [not] the external award and determination of men" should guide in interpreting them (W.P. II:7).

"Take away Revelation and the Gospel ceases . . . and the most excellent part of the Scriptures, God's Traditions, is made void." (W.P. II:221) "The Book is sealed, the Scriptures are unknown" without "that holy Principle which leads to it and in it." (W.P. II:211) "The first Protestants" charged the Roman Catholic Church "with making God's Tradition (the holy Scriptures) void by their numerous . . . traditions." (W.P. II:206) "Venturing to wade into the holy Scriptures without this divine Principle . . . has caused so many fearful miscarriages about religion. . . . Man . . . hastily spoils all with the intermixture of his own fancies and conceits . . . [and] he sticks not to style his own inventions 'orthodox.'" (W.P. II:205)

"It is . . . the sum of Scripture prophecy" that God makes himself known "by the Spirit of his Son" to any who "hear his heavenly Voice and knocks, and let him in, and be taught of him to know and do his Will. . . . Unless this be man's rule and judge in the reading and believing . . . of the Scriptures of Truth . . . he can never understand them rightly." (W.P. II:25-26)

"Weigh it whether anything can give to understand aright . . . but God's Light, Grace, or Word in the heart . . . Christ's pure, unerring Light in the conscience (Jn. 8:12. 1 Jn. 1:5-7) . . . is sufficient to daily understanding and duty . . . [and will] not suffer themselves to be carried away with the torrent of fathers, councils, synods, doctors, scholars, national constitutions, etc." (W.P. II:206-207). "The smallness of the writings of the Evangelists, the shortness of Christ's sermons" contrast with "the many and great volumes of commentators and critics. . . . The text is almost lost in the comment." (W.P. III:54)

"Emmanuel, God with men, as he is their rule, so their judge: he is the lawgiver, and therefor the best interpreter of any point that may concern his own law: and men are so far certain as they are subject to his Voice, Light, or Spirit in them, and no farther," man by himself "is errable." (W.P. II:22)

(5) All of the Bible and all statements on any one subject should be taken into account:

"The Scriptures . . . seem not . . . to have been compiled and delivered as the general rule, and entire body of faith, but rather written upon particular occasions and emergencies." (W.P. II:5) The Bible is not to be appealed to without some discrimination. Samuel Fisher criticized the Puritans for collecting proof texts "by wholesale more than by retail." And although he was willing to allow that there could be such a thing as a "most capital and cardinal text" he was also ready to deride any "grand master place . . . used for proof" that did not measure up. (Samuel Fisher *Works* pp. BG 52, 72 and main numbering, pp. 442 and 646)

At the same time one could derive basic principles from words of the Bible by examining them to see, for example, if they had anything comparable to the lengthy and verbose proclamations of the great Ecumenical Councils. Instead of these, "a short creed of words served of old [along] with an upright heart: 'Thou art the Son of God. Thou art the King of Israel,' was Nathaniel's confession. 'My Lord and my God,' was all of Thomas's retraction and creed, John 20:28, and Peter's confession of faith is little larger (Mt. 16:16). To be a Christian then was to be like Christ: meek, humble, holy, loving, patient: and this his Light and Spirit maketh those that embrace it." (W.P. III:264-265) experiential, legal, or narrative in character should all enter into the process of interpretation.

Nonetheless, "weighing the text, consulting the intent of the writer, comparing places together" is a useful, but a fallible way of interpreting the Bible. It is "the Spirit of God 'which gives understanding'" Job 32:8 and 1 Corinthians 2:11, and "searcheth the deep things of God." (W.P. II:22)

Still it is useful to remember "*kai* being here explicative" (W.P. II:227); and "they tell us that the Greek particle *en* is often to be translated 'among,'" rather than "to" you or "in" you, as should be the case with Colossians 1:27 and other places allowed by us. (Robert Barclay & George Keith "Q'm Confirmed," in Robert Barclay *Works,* p. 602)

This argument continues to this day, but it was the KJV, not the Quakers, that translated *en* as "among" 114 times; "into, to" or "unto" 35 times, and "in" 1,863 times.

Things change. The practice of "Jacob, Esau, David, etc. . . . is not our rule." The times are different. We are under the Gospel and New Covenant. The sphere of application of texts differs, too; some texts apply to "morals," others to "fiducials" – that is, matters of faith (S.F. *Works,* p. BG 83). Fisher is also aware of "metonymy" (pp. 105, 509, 524) and of "metaphor." (p. 527) He also distinguishes between a more or less built-in sense, a "*sensu architectonico,*" and a "*sensum forensam,*" one that is open to, or requires, arguing as in a court of law. (p. 510)

"Take not that strictly which is spoken with construction; nor that properly or literally which is figuratively and mystically expressed, or to be understood" in that way. (W.P. III:259) There are also "types and antitypes, shadows and substances, parables, and morals." (W.P. II:231) And "Christ is called a door . . . a lion . . . a vine . . . and lastly he calls himself by the name of bread, because of that inward strength and nourishment such receive that feed spiritually upon him." (W.P. II:232)

"We shall not refuse learning where it may perform the office of an honest servant, not an usurper." (W.P. II:228)

(7) There is an experiential dimension to the Bible. Not only do these "holy writings . . . possess more than earthly beauty" they are redemptive, imparting "strength and hope":

"Parrots may learn Scripture, but can never experience it. And those . . . who know not by experience . . . are unprofitable canters, indeed, who confidently talk of what they never felt." (W.P. II:222) Some "have the Scriptures, true; but the 'word of canters, indeed, who confidently talk of what they never felt." (W.P. II:222) Some "have the Scriptures, true; but the 'word of reconciliation that brings to God'" they lack. "Their heads know, but do their hearts feel the operation of that Truth they will sometimes in words declare? Have they travelled the Way, and traced the many anxious steps of that New Birth which is the only door into the heavenly Kingdom?" (W.P. II:260) "You profess the holy Scriptures; but what do you witness and experience? What interest have you in them? Can you set to your seal [that] they are true, by the work of the same Spirit in you that gave them forth in the holy ancients?" (W.P. II:338) "Consider if it be not the bare or mere man, that speaks of godly matters what he has heard, or read, of others' labors rather than the overshadowings and operations of the holy and eternal Spirit of Christ in yourselves." (W.P. II:373) "Without that great agent, the Spirit, influencing and enabling the creature, he shall never experience the truth of the Scriptures to himself." (W.P. III:250) Only "that divine Principle . . . can clear up their understandings, and give them experimental [that is, 'experiential'] knowledge of the true God." (W.P. II:207) It is by the "convictions and operations of God's Grace in the conscience" that all "that Christ did without [is] brought nigh and home to the very soul . . . Christ the Light and Lamb does not only . . . take away the sins [of the] past . . . but cleanses from the nature, root, and ground of sin." (W.P. II:208)

(8) In preparation for the guidance of the Spirit of Christ, variant readings of the text of the Bible, and various versions [or translations] should be consulted, as well as commentaries:

Penn refers to two translations. First, he speaks of the "Bible imprinted Ann. 1559, in quarto." Presumably he means the Geneva Bible, which was on the presses in that year, although it was not issued until 1569. The other reference is to the "Folio Bible, printed Ann. 1578." This was "the first large folio edition" of the Geneva Bible, as identified by the marginal note he quotes in expansion of Matthew 5:34's "Swear not at all." It reads: "Let simplicity and truth be in your words, and then ye shall not be so light and so ready to swear."

There is also a reference by Barclay to George "Pasor, whose translation" an opponent charged them with "following in one thing, but not another." (R.B. *Works* p. 72). According to Bruce Metzger, Pasor was author of "the first grammar of the Greek NT," but he knows of no translation by Pasor. I am indebted to him for a search for one.

Tyndale's translation is mentioned in connection with the meaning of the word "church": "What is this 'church,' or 'congregation' rather (as worthy Tindal everywhere translates it)? . . . The word 'church' signifies any assembly; so the Greeks used it." (W.P. III:101, 106)

"Various lections," or variant readings, are referred to at a number of points. "The variety of readings which we find amongst those copies . . . [and] it were to be wished we knew which were nighest to the original . . . [amounts] to several thousands." (W.P. II:7)

The variations in the text were being much discussed in England because of the London Polyglot Bible, which had been published by Bp. Walton in 1657. This included variants excerpted by Thomas Pierce from the *Annotations* of Hugo Grotius. These appeared in vol. 6, as Penn duly notes adding the correct title for that portion of the work, "variae lectiones graec. nov. test." (W.P. II:7).

Barclay's *Apology* has numerous references to the heaps of commentaries that had been written through the centuries, a single reference from Penn probably suffices here: "Many orders of Christians . . . unite in the text, and differ only in the comment; all owning one Deity, Savior, and Judge; [as well as] good works, rewards and punishments." (W.P. II:539)

Chapter 8

THE TRIUNITY OF GOD

Few areas of Christian theology have been the subject of as much controversy or have developed as many "safeguards" as thought about God. All seven of the first Councils regarded as ecumenical by the Orthodox Churches (ending with Nicaea II in A.D. 787) devoted much of their efforts to hammering out Creeds for coping with divergent interpretations of the Godhead.

The targets of all this activity were a baker's dozen of heresies that proposed "unorthodox" views of God. Some denied the divinity of Christ (Docetism and Arianism), the reality of His humanity (Phantasiasm and Monophysitism), the real unity of His divine and human natures (Nestorianism), or that He had a human will (Monothelitism). Others would have subordinated Him to God, whose Son they considered Him only by adoption rather than by nature (Subordination or Adoptionism). One found no connection at all between the God of the Christians and the God of the Jews (Marcionism). Still others denied the divinity of the Holy Spirit (Macedonianism) or that Father, Son, and Holy Spirit were really distinct divine persons, viewing them instead as three different modes of Being and ways of Self-manifestation (Monarchianism, Patripassianism, Sabellianism).

Not only did three major Creeds emerge from the proceedings of these early Councils, but the Creeds were surrounded by and embedded in a Doctrine of the Trinity believed to be the perfect solution to the God problem, and the "most sublime mystery of the Christian faith." The "holy Trinity" was commemorated by a votive mass dating from the seventh century, and an Office composed for it in the tenth century. It became a "feast" extended to the universal Church in the fourteenth century. Later, churches were given the name Holy Trinity, and a triangular diagram of the relationship between the "persons" became a permanent fixture adorning the walls or stained-glass windows of many a church building.

Yet, in spite of all the claims made for this way of dealing with the Triunity of God, it is a far from perfect solution. Arthur W. Wainwright, in examining the New Testament for Trinitarian emphases, prefers to speak of the "problem," rather than the "doctrine" of the Trinity, because "there is no formal statement of the doctrine of the Trinity in the New Testament." Even the word on which "Trinity" is based "does not appear to have emerged before Theophilus (second century), who used the Greek *trias* ('triad') to describe Father, Son, and Holy Spirit; or before Tertullian, who used the Latin *trinitas* [beginning of the third century] for the same purpose."[1] The Quaker patristician and biblical scholar, J. Rendel Harris, regarded something as "gained by the admission that evolution is really a factor in Christian belief." He credits Cardinal John Henry Newman, whose theory of the development of doctrine has been almost universally accepted, with putting the onus on those who believe "that things have always been the same from the first, to study carefully how they came to be so different from what they were at the beginning."[2] At any rate, returning to Wainwright, in spite of all the creativity lavished on it, "the Trinitarian problem . . . has never been satisfactorily answered." Even "the most enduring statements of the doctrine do not give complete answers . . . but [instead] define the limits of discussion."[3]

The Situation Today

In actual fact, most theologians perform a balancing act and walk a tightrope above the various heresies. In their constructions each "person" of the Trinity is assigned a "correct" share of the duties of the Godhead. But in spite of all this attention given to the Triunity of the Godhead, many of the points at issue in the early heresies were repeated in the Middle Ages and had to be recondemned. And modern theologians find tightrope walking in a sort of metaphysical stratosphere a difficult feat even where zero-gravity from mundane considerations prevails. A work as recent as 1981 states: "The number one problem for the theologian remains the problem of God."[4] This statement no more than updates by a few years another that "perhaps the clearest indication of the radical nature of today's theological endeavor is the fact that the question of God has come center stage."[5]

To use a broad brush for a moment and paint with a bit of tongue in cheek, much of Protestantism tends to relapse into a Christomonism. On the other hand, both Eastern Orthodoxy and Roman Catholicism long ago added a celestial nobility to the heavenly hierarchy of Father, Son, and Spirit. From their positions of special privilege the Blessed Virgin and the Saints perpetually espouse the cause of time-bound earthlings before the heavenly throne. At the same time, Christ's "divinity" tends to be overemphasized at the expense of His "humanity." Another type of imbalance is found in some quarters of modern Quakerism where the Spirit fails to reflect a close tie with Christ. In this distortion of the early Quaker understanding, where Christ and Spirit were almost interchangeable and most certainly inseparable where matters of Presence were concerned, a vulnerability to theistic or pantheistic interpretations develops.

In practice, the Holy Spirit's role can range ecumenically from a ghostly Presence in nearly every aspect of the Eastern Orthodox liturgy and ecclesiastical practice to lip service, which in reality amounts to a near absence in most Protestant thought. The "high churches" as a group were suddenly startled out of a complacent reminiscing about the Holy Spirit by an invasion from the Pentecostal movement; however the Pentecostal churches themselves confine the role of the Spirit largely to orchestrating the speaking of tongues in the spiritually baptized. Until recently, in the Roman Catholic Church the Spirit was treated as a sort of distant ancestor who was enthroned publicly on Conciliar occasions and confined largely to the cloister at other times. Yet, in spite of this proclivity, Catholicism nevertheless succeeded in constructively "domesticating" the wild, new, and renewing dynamic unleashed by the Pentecostals. Other churches reached by Pentecostalism were not always as successful, and the heavy winds of the Spirit sometimes created new divisions.

God the Father, in spite of the close and intimate parallels with earthly fathers stressed by Jesus of Nazareth (especially in his use of *Abba,* "dad," or even "daddy"), tended to be for many a cold philosophical construction or a derivation from Old Testament partriarchalism. Furthermore, even where the Father has "equal time," so to speak, in Christian theology, He tends to have merely a preparatory or preliminary role as Creator, rather than as Redeemer.

A vast literature has accumulated in attempting to cope with the problem of language about "God" and its inability to reach the modern mind and spirit effectively. In one discussion metaphysics or dogma is the culprit. In another it is supernaturalism, or again, an overemphasis on immanence as opposed to transcendence. Nevertheless there is a tremendous search for new metaphors, analogies, and parables or other forms of narrative to restore theistic imagery to the consciousness of the secularly and technologically oriented.

Recently the hazards of neutron technology, among other things, have tended to detract from the awe in which science was held for some time. It is not too long ago that Raimundo Panikkar made a statement that still has a ring of some truth about it[6]: "This primacy of data is still visible in the last of human activities to handle the real. The natural sciences, in fact, are still almost in ecstasies under the spell of the data, here called scientific facts." The empirical approach of science, however, is not the whole answer to existence. Panikkar broadens the horizons of existential observation, creating as his frame of reference what he calls "the cosmotheandric vision of reality," and which he finds "an almost universal cultural invariant." He goes on to say that he "can capsulize the cosmotheandric principle, which I have developed at length elsewhere, by noting that *the divine, the human, and the earthly* – however we prefer to call them – are three real and different dimensions that constitute the real, i.e., any reality inasmuch as it is real."[7]

In another treatise, Fr. Panikkar has stated: "Any human problem today that is not put thematically over against the global human horizon is bound to remain at the surface . . . touching neither the heart of the matter nor the shores of the divine . . . . Nowhere does one suffer more from what St. Thomas . . . called the *inopia vocabulorum,* the misery of terms," precisely when he was writing on nothing other than the Trinity.[8] Panikkar's own book on the Trinity was written as "an invitation to enter that path in which the divine depths and the human heights meet; where the necessary distinctions between philosophy and theology, matter and spirit, reason and faith, God and man, one religious tradition and another, are not blurred; but where they do not become lethal separations either."[9] Such an approach may be above the head of many Christians, but it will hardly seem aimed at infantile or escapist mentalities.

Other recent formulations often seem to add more to the complexities of the problem than they do to the solution. A contributing factor to this is the difference in theological orientation between East and West, whose divergent "approaches to the Doctrine of the Trinity go back to the Patristic period. The entire Patristic tradition of the East has a 'personalistic' approach . . . whereas in the West St. Augustine authored the so-called 'psychological' approach."[10] Furthermore, "the West was more conceptual, more haunted by precision. It mistrusted metaphors and looked rather for proper analogies."[11] Yet, in spite of the obscurities and problems that have been mentioned, and although "the Fathers certainly have not exhausted in their writings all the potentialities and implications of theology . . . the further one penetrates in the depth of their experience of the Triune God, the more implications one discovers for the solution of our own problems."[12]

A conservative Roman Catholic theologian, Leslie Dewart, has stated: "The Doctrine of the Trinity, the absolutely basic doctrine of the Christian faith, has through undevelopment become inadequate to the point that it must be seriously suspected of causing some scandal—not simply that of incredibility but that of irrelevance and senselessness."[13] Another Catholic with a long history of ecumenical involvement, George Tavard, has one of the most recent surveys of both the history and problems of Trinitarian doctrine. He states that the motive behind his study "is simply the conviction that the vision of the Three is central to the Christian understanding of God and style of living, and that the nucleus of contemporary theological research should be, not revision of past positions for the sake of updating Christian thought in the eyes of our contemporaries, and not even human liberation; but God, as God is experienced in Christian life and as this experience is or ought to be projected into theology."[14]

Fr. Tavard's explorations of the bases of Trinitarian thought raise the question of whether the very structure of meaning may not be bifocal or trifocal although the present writer cannot help but wonder whether some efforts to locate such numerical universals are merely attempts to find significance of a higher sort in what are nothing more than simple cultural pattern numbers. He would ask whether an anthropologist like Levi-Strauss may not have lost touch with everyday reality (or perhaps his bearings) when he proposes, be it said, in Tavard's words, not his own, "two basic models for society, a dual model on the male-female pattern and a three-fold model on the pattern of raw-rotten-cooked in eating habits!"[15] In spite of this excursus, however, Fr. Tavard's conclusion offers a hint of another major dimension that needs to be incorporated into any restructuring of doctrine about the Triunity of God: "The Doctrine of the Trinity, as I have tried to show, finds its depth in the fact that it is primarily a vision. Only a vision can awaken the hopes that lie dormant in the human soul. Only a vision can lead humankind to a really new future."[16]

Trinitarian Discussion in the Seventeenth Century

Little more can be claimed for the seventeenth century criticisms of the early Friends than a general muddying of the waters. Nonetheless, they were among the forerunners of what in the twentieth century has become an overwhelming tide of criticism of standard Trinitarian doctrine. The late Geoffrey Lampe, Regius Professor of Divinity at Cambridge, probably summarized the questioning most sharply, and a bit ironically, when he stated: "What future is there for the . . . *doctrine* of the Trinity? I am bound to reply, even within these walls of Trinity College, 'Not much.'"[17] Unfortunately, however, since Christians of so many varieties recite the Nicean Creed and the Chalcedonian formulations in which the doctrine is imbedded, these cannot realistically be revised until a genuinely Ecumenical Council can be convened.

One church, or even a group of churches, can do no more than update the translations of these widely used statements. Actually that was done by the International Committee on English in the Liturgy several years ago. All of its proposals except the new version of the Lord's Prayer (which pleased no one) have been widely adopted.

Even though little positive can be claimed for the way in which the early Friends stated their rejection of the standard Creeds and Trinitarian doctrine, it should be made clear that their objections were neither simplistic, nor unitarian, nor agnostic. Most importantly, they did not object to what it was that these symbols were trying to convey. They did object to the metaphysical terminology that was used, and to the overemphasis on the professing aspect of faith that their constant use represented.

Their criticism was especially aimed at the recital of the Creeds by rote. This seemed to add little to the apprehension and appropriation of them in personal experience, witness, and daily practice. True knowledge of God should not be solely intellectual, but "it should involve one's whole life and one's whole strength" if there is to be "even a modest awareness of spiritual realities."[18]

Barclay does not seem to have gotten into these debates over the Trinity and the Creeds, so we shall have to turn to our other early Quakers for explicit discussion. Even though he does not seem to have authored anything concerned explicitly with these topics, their substance played a major part in his theology. We can round out some of the basis from which he obviously wrote by turning to these contemporary spokesmen.

Samuel Fisher, for example, criticized those who were constantly "talking . . . of Christ, the Son of God, yet refusing to hear His Voice, when He speaks to them in their own malicious hearts." This was not only "empty profession without the possession of that Godliness ye prate of,"[19] but a refusal to become "his disciples in deed and not in word only."[20] Even in 1660 there were "English nominal Christians of all forms and professions."[21] Barclay adds to this criticism of nominalism that many remain in darkness "notwithstanding all their professions and confessions of him." They constitute great "dry mountains of dead professions and observations" and are without the Life of Christianity.[22]

Criticisms of Theological Language

One of the most concise critiques of the language in which the Creeds were couched is that of William Penn. He makes it clear that he is not objecting to what they were trying to convey. "We plainly and entirely believe," he said, "the truths contained in the Creed that is commonly called 'the Apostles.'"[23] He went even further: "Except it be the wording of some of the Articles of Faith in School-terms, there are very few of them professed by the Church of England to which we do not heartily assent."

Penn continues: "It is generally thought that we do not hold the common doctrines of Christianity, but have introduced new and erroneous ones in lieu thereof." Not only "do we own [i.e., affirm or acknowledge] the Christian faith" so far as already explained, but could even affirm it "in all points" as it is expressed "in the Creed commonly called the Athanasian; except that about the Trinity, which seems to me to be less plain by that copious way taken to explain it."[24]

If Penn criticized the "copiousness" of the Athanasian words for tending to make its doctrine less obvious, he is far from being alone today. Not only the criticisms we have already cited, but as conservative a modern work as *The Common Catechism* admits that in relation to the Chalcedonian formulations, "Christians, in every century, have had trouble in understanding what the

Church was saying—as can be seen from the tortuous labors of theology after 451."[25]

The early Creeds are usually presented as necessary to forestall misconstruction of doctrine, and as having settled the disputes that brought them about. But the standard history of *The Doctrine of the Trinity,* by R.S. Franks, points out that Athanasius found it necessary to devote his whole life to defending the Nicean Creed. This was necessary because the coalition by which all but two of the bishops had signed the Creed soon broke up. Three parties emerged once the influence of the Emperor (who had called the Council) waned and the desire for peace lessened. The Arians proper held that the Logos (Christ, the Word) was unlike the Father. A few Eastern Homoöusians remained faithful to the similarity and were supported by the West. But Eusebius of Caesarea was typical of the vast majority in the Eastern Church who preferred to say that the Word was "of like essence with the Father," rather than "of the same essence."[26]

Today these differences seem to be rather tedious hairsplitting, and many suspect the Creed's defenders "of merely reproducing no longer feasible 'mythologies.'"[27] One commentator, indeed, has referred to the use of Scholastic concepts (which might perhaps be extended to metaphysical terminology as well) as "The intellectual incest of merely quoting our predecessors of happy memory. "

Unfortunately, too, the modern psychologically influenced notion of person tends to cause us to see each divine "person" as having an independent center of consciousness. Father Capon, an Episcopalian, has caricatured this well: "Let me tell you," he says, "why God made the world. One afternoon, before anything was made, God the Father, God the Son, and God the Holy Ghost sat around in the unity of their Godhead discussing . . . ."[28]

Yet "what is at stake here," in this doctrine of the Triunity of God, "is not the magical power of the number 'three'";[29] nor is it "a mere game with words. The whole theology is determined by the doctrines of the Trinity, Grace, and Incarnation—doctrines which mutually condition one another."[30] Yet "the form which it [the theology of the Trinity] took on during the first 1500 years . . . has scarcely been modified in the last 500." And "no important progress or changes have come in the kerygmatic statement or religious practice . . . [related to the Triunity of God since] the Athanasian Creed and the Council of Florence."[31]

Margaret Hobling has written: "To the seventeenth century Quakers the thought of God as Father, Son and Holy Spirit was no mere 'notion,' no adventurous sally of the speculative faculty into the unknown: it lay at the basis of their whole religious life. The God whom they claimed to know in their own experience – 'experimentally' or 'sensibly,' as they expressed it – was known to them as Father, Son and Holy Spirit."[32]

"Mistake me not," said William Penn, "We never have disowned a Father, Word, and Spirit, which are one." What we have "utterly rejected" as "heathenish metaphysics" is the "men's inventions" that "have been introduced."[33] This kind of man-made philosophical conceptualization in theology was disavowed by all the early Friends. Neither the philosophers nor the rabbinical scholars improved Scripture, Fisher said, by adding their "own thoughts, inventions, and imaginations" or by making "their own senses, meanings and traditionary interpretations of the Letter."[34]

Whenever the subject of the Triunity of God came up the early Friends would cite 1 John 5:7 KJV: "For there are three that bear record in heaven, the Father, the Word, and the Holy Ghost: and these three are one." But even in their day the authenticity of this text was doubted, as Margaret Hobling has shown. The United Bible Societies *Textual Commentary* goes even further. It says that all the words that follow "bear record," in verse 7 are "spurious and have no right to stand in the New Testament."[35]

Although this is the only scriptural text that comes close to full trinitarianism, its removal does not take away all of the "raw material" for developing a doctrine of Triunity. Indeed, Samuel Fisher mentioned 2 Cor. 3; 1 Cor. 15:45; Rev. 19:13, and Eph. 6:17 in addition to the usual 1 John 5:7.[36] Robert Barclay expressly and unhesitatingly stated: "That we deny the thing truly imported by the Trinity is false."[37] Barclay regarded Scholasticism and syllogistic reasoning as "vain jangling" even though he sometimes used both to "prove" a point.[38] Fisher termed the Scholastic method a "syllogistical siege"[39] and a "species of magic." He asked one of his disputants not to tell him "of Thomas, of John Duns the Scot, and other skeptics, Schoolmen, and casuists, that make religion a matter of dispute more than practice.[40] "This 'science,' so-called," he said, "is more like a mixture of superstitious Athenians, university philosophers, Epicureans and Stoics, who worship an unknown God."[41] They are "dunces . . . in the School of Christ."[42]

"True theology," Fisher said, "is plain to Godly-hearted honest men in the Scripture."[43] It needs none of the "twistings and turnings, and choppings and changings, and piecings and patchings, and shiftings and shufflings" that lead "away from Truth."[44]

Just to prove that Quakers knew how to "do metaphysics," so to speak, Fisher wrote an essay on God. It has a certain freshness about it that makes it worth quoting: "What is God really in himself . . . in the broadest sense? And in what did he dwell and manifest himself before the foundation of the heavens and the earth was laid? God as he really is in himself is beyond all definition . . . Description . . . [would] be intruding into things which ye have not seen. God is really . . . whatever he hath in and by his Son revealed himself to be, in and to his holy Prophets and Children, whether by word of mouth or Scripture. And so whatever ye there read; God is *that* God. [He] is really in deed and in Truth a Spirit, Light, Love, that one omnipotent, all-suffering, all-sufficient, Spiritual, substantial, living, ever-lasting, infinite Substance, which hath his own Being of himself, and gives being, life, breath and all things unto all."[45]

Fox spoke of "notions"—as theological concepts were then frequently referred to—as "men's inventions and windy doctrines, by which they blowed the people about, this way and the other way, from sect to sect."[46] "The Life and Truth will outlast all airy notions."[47]

Whenever Friends were to witness or minister to their faith, Fox's advice was "to keep to Scripture-language, terms, words and doctrines . . . in matters of faith, religion, controversy and conversation"; and do not be "drawn into unscriptural terms" or allow them "to be imposed upon" such discussions.[48]

Yet with 1 John 5:27 declared spurious, Penn's question whether there is "a plainer, or a fuller [statement] anywhere in the writings of the New Testament" of the Triunity of God becomes a dead issue. Without that text to rely upon some fresh statement of the Triunity of God is needed. At least *part* of the basis for reformulation can be found in the early Quaker writings, but if it is to be enlisted for such a purpose, it needs to be made explicit. When the time comes for all Christians to revise this area of theology together, Friends have what could well be an important contribution if an adequate forum and competent spokespersons can be found.

Reformulation of the Triunity of God

Whatever content is given to any ecumenically oriented reformulation, it would be well to include as a subsidiary statement what Roman Catholic theology has called "circumincession." That strange word means that where reference is made to one member of the Trinity, the others are also assumed to be present. Not only would this prevent theistic or pantheistic aberrations; it would make it more difficult to misinterpret statements that refer to only one member of the Godhead. The basic principle behind circumincession is that where only one member of the Godhead has been named, the most appropriate name for that particular function or attribute has been chosen. Without a circumincession proviso, there are many times when a statement could be seen solely in terms of theology proper, Christology, or Pneumatology—three Gods rather than three aspects of the One God.

Any Quaker contribution to reformulation would almost certainly contain some reference to the Light, Spirit, Grace, enablement and empowerment of Christ Jesus. In that aspect of Christology Friends excelled their contemporaries in the seventeenth century, and even today few theologies are as well developed in that area. One difference between the seventeenth and twentieth centuries is that few critics today would construe their talk about Light as referring to a "natural light." Yet in the seventeenth century when neo-Platonism enjoyed some popularity, their language was apt to suggest the terms of the "natural theology," which served as a foundation for "revealed theology."

Out of this context, Penn offers what could well be an appropriate starting point for a modern doctrine of Triunity, although this kind of two-story theology is not as common or as well received today. It is remarkable that although Penn's terminology is different, he affirms what Karl Rahner has called the close relationship between "the doctrines of Trinity, Grace, and Incarnation." And Penn's starting point, if not "anthropological existential"—to use Rahner's most characteristic description of his own theology—is certainly immanental-yet-transcendental in its implications.

"The Light," Penn said, "is nothing other than a manifestation in the soul of man, of Christ, 'the Word of God, the Light of the world, the second Adam, the Lord from heaven, the quickening Spirit, who was full of Grace and Truth; and of whom man hath received' . . . a talent, a proportion [of Grace] suitable to his want and capacity, to convince and to convert him, to renew and restore him . . . again."[49]

Raimundo Panikkar has stated:[50] "The message of Christ is a message of freedom; it carries the freedom requisite to perform the free act that saves. It is clear, moreover, that only an interior Christ (which does not deny a historical Christ identified with him) can make possible the realization of an act that is truly free, spontaneous, and fully human; otherwise it would just be a new imposition from outside . . . . The Gospel is a good and joyful news . . . . It announces freedom, not an objective dehumanized – not to say inhuman – freedom; but a concrete, real, existential freedom to each man's personal measure."

Notes to Chapter 8

1. Arthur W. Wainwright, *The Trinity in the New Testament* (London:SPCK, 1962) pp. vii & 4.
2. Rendel Harris, *The Origin of the Doctrine of the Trinity: A Popular Exposition* (Manchester: University Press, 1919), pp. 9-10.
3. Wainwright, *op. cit.*, p. 5.
4. Deane William Ferm, *Contemporary American Theologies – A Critical Survey* (New York: Seabury, 1981), p. ix.
5. Bernard J. Cooke, S.J. *Beyond Trinity,* Aquinas Lecture, 1969 (Milwaukee: Marquette University Press, 1969), p. 2.
6. R. Panikkar, *Myth, Faith and Hermeneutics – Cross-Cultural Studies* (Ramsay, NJ: Paulist Press, 1979), p. 295.
7. Panikkar, *op. cit.*, pp. 136-137.
8. Raimundo Panikkar, *The Trinity and the Religious Experience of Man: Icon-Person-Mystery* (Maryknoll, NY: Orbis, 1973), pp. vii & viii.
9. *Ibid.*, p. xiv.
10. Michael A. Fahey and John Meyendorff, *Trinitarian Theology East and West: St. Thomas Aquinas – St. Gregory Palamas,* Patriarch Athenagoras Memorial Lectures (Brookline, MA: Holy Cross Orthodox Press, 1979), from the Foreword by Maximos Aghiorgoussis, p. 2.
11. Fahey and Meyendorff, *op. cit.*, from Michael A. Fahey, S.J. "Trinitarian Theology in Thomas Aquinas: One Latin Medieval Pursuit of Word and Silence," p. 19.
12. Fahey and Meyendorff, *op. cit.*, from John Meyendorff, "The Holy Trinity in Palamite Theology," p. 42.
13. Leslie Dewart, *The Future of Belief: Theism in a World Come of Age* (New York: Herder and Herder, 1966), p. 144.
14. George H. Tavard, *The Vision of the Trinity* (Washington: University Press of America, 1981), pp. vii-viii.
15. Tavard, *op. cit.*, p. 146.
16. *Ibid.*, p. 148.
17. G.W.H. Lampe, "What Future for the Trinity?" chapter 3 of his *Explorations in Theology 8* (London: SCM, 1981) p. 30. (Italics in original).
18. Tavard, *op. cit.*, p. 93.
19. Samuel Fisher, *Works*, p. 148.
20. *Ibid.*, p. 712.
21. *Ibid.*, p. 828.
22. Robert Barclay, *Works*, (London: Northcott, 1692) pp. 11, 5.
23. Wm. Penn, *Works*, (London: Phillips, 1825) III:576.

24. *Ibid.*, III: 547, 576, 583.
25. *The Common Catechism* ed. by Johannes Feiner and Lukas Vischer (New York: Seabury, 1975), p. 256.
26. R. S. Franks, *The Doctrine of the Trinity* (London: Duckworth, 1953), p. 107.
27. Karl Rahner, S.J. "Theology and Anthropology," *Theological Investigations* (London: Darton, Longman & Todd, 1972), vol. 9, p. 28.
28. Robert Farrar Capon, *The Third Peacock: The Goodness of God and the Badness of the World* (New York: Doubleday-Image, 1972), p. 11.
29. Carl E. Braaten, *The Future of God: The Revolutionary Dynamics of Hope* (New York: Harper & Row, 1969), p. 106.
30. Taped notes from a lecture by Karl Rahner.
31. Karl Rahner, S.J. "Trinity in Theology," *Sacramentum Mundi*, vol. 6, pp. 307, 303-304.
32. Margaret B. Hobling, "Early Friends and the Doctrine of the Trinity," in *Then and Now*, ed. by Anna Brinton (Philadelphia: University of Pennsylvania Press, 1960), p. 119.
33. Penn, "The Sandy Foundation Shaken" (1668), *Works* I: 134, 153.
34. Fisher, *Works*, p. 704.
35. Bruce M. Metzger, *A Textual Commentary on the Greek New Testament* (Stuttgart: United Bible Societies, 1971), p. 716.
36. Fisher, *Works*, p. 499.
37. Barclay, *"Apology* Vindicated" (1679), *Works*, p. 855.
38. Barclay, *Works*, p. 730.
39. Fisher, *Works*, pp. 205, 265.
40. *Ibid.*, p. 154.
41. *Ibid.*, pp. 207, 2.
42. *Ibid.*, p. 436.
43. *Ibid.*, p. 459.
44. *Ibid.*, p. 283.
45. *Ibid.*, p. 844.
46. George Fox, *Journal*, revised edition by John L. Nickalls (Cambridge: University Press, 1952), p. 36.
47. George Fox, *Journal*, Bi-Centenary edition (London, 1891), II: 309.
48. Second-Day-Morning Meeting Epistle, prefaced to Fox's *Doctrinals* (London: Sowle, 1706) pages unnumbered.
49. Penn, "A Defense of a Paper, Entitled Gospel Truths, Against the Exceptions of the Bishop of Cork's Testimony" (1698), *Works* III: 552.
50. R. Panikkar, *Myth, Faith, and Hermeneutics—Cross-Cultural Studies* (Ramsey, NJ: Paulist Press, 1979), pp. 453-454.

Chapter 9

MAKING ROOM FOR THE GRACE OF GOD

One does an injustice to the practice of early Friends and misconstrues their theology as well if the place of spiritual discipline in their lives is ignored. One of the many contributions of Father Nesti's fine study of first-generation Quakerism[1] is that he calls attention to this. He states that the righteousness and holiness, which so marked their lives, was not only "far from easy to live and sustain," but it required "a highly developed asceticism."

"Asceticism" is a term little used by Quakers, but if it is to be *a propos* it must be properly defined, and one must also keep in mind their distrust of ritualization of practices or setting up a calendar of religious observances. The early Friends utterly rejected anything that smacked of "man's inventions" in such matters. When they fasted, or withdrew from active pursuits in the hope of spiritual refreshment, or acted nonresistantly, this was not done to influence God or to win religious or political quarrels. Whatever was done of this nature was intended to eliminate any self-interest and self-will so that Christ might be free to guide and rule directly – to "teach his people himself."

The Work of Christ

A brief review of some of Christ's sanctifying and redeeming work should help to clarify the contributory role of ascetical practices and it may help to resolve what has long been a problem for modern Quakerism. I refer to the tension between prophetism and mysticism. If a basis for holding these together creatively and constructively can be found, they should interact to renew and revivify an obsolescing faith and perhaps transform it into a modern Quakerhood.

To class the apologists—particularly Barclay and Penington—as apostate, or at least as opening the door to later apostasy, because of their insistence on a mystical aspect to Quakerism, in my judgment leads to the discrediting of something very important. The interest in mysticism and the mystical aspect of Quaker beliefs and practices—although I am far from judging Quakers "Mystics" in any classical sense of the term—is a rich heritage that has contributed much of the uniqueness to this form of Christianity.

Furthermore, what seems at first glance to be grossly simple—particularly if one's observations begin with an uninformed look at unprogrammed worship—actually involves a complex of *a priori* attitudes and practices. These give shape and meaning to what would otherwise be mere silent meditation, or at best a rather formless and somewhat random unmediated encounter with Christ.

The initial work of the Light/Grace of Christ, and the necessary prelude to any rebirth or transformation, is "conviction"—a revelatory insight into what is wrong in one's behavior, or what stems from evil. I am going to propose that it might be helpful to confine the Light/Grace terminology to the work of "Sanctification," and to limit the use of Voice metaphors to dealing with Christ's prophetic guidance in Mission. While the documentary evidence (on a somewhat less than exhaustive examination) does not seem to indicate that the early Friends made such a separation, that would not prevent us from doing so if it proved helpful in our own situation.

Similarly, because Fox or some other early Friend sometimes mixed metaphors, e.g., in saying that "the Light speaks," or asking Friends to "hear the Light" is no reason why we have to do so. Mixed metaphors of this kind seem illogical to us and are inconsistent with our usage in everyday speech. They are also as irritating in some respects as the seemingly endless repetition that Fox sometimes used to hammer home a point.[2]

The visual metaphors seem more appropriate for the less "personal" work of Grace in transforming lives and characters, while voice metaphors seem better suited to the role of Christ as divine Prophet, where the major thrust is to promote faithfulness or offer guidance in putting God's will into practice. The Old Testament Prophets were continually calling Israel to task whenever the people of God failed to apply faith justly, equitably, and above all righteously. The role of the New Testament Prophets seems to have been closely related. The New Testament Prophet has primary responsibility for vocal ministry and for charting the Way ahead under the Inspiration of the Spirit and lordship of Christ. The Way they advocated is that which Christ still calls us to follow if we "have ears to hear."

Barclay states that merely talking about the life of Christ on earth will not redeem us in the sight of God. We must allow His Light to lead us from the love of this world into truth and holiness. To do so requires taking up the cross of Christ and dying to the lusts and perishable vanities of this world. *[437]* Under the gospel dispensation "those who want to be disciples of Christ" are commanded "to be more perfect and exemplary," nothing less than "the complete personification of Christian love." *[426]* To achieve such "perfection," one must be "leavened with the love of God" and filled with the "sense of His Presence." *[410]*

Mortification/"Asceticism"

Concomitant with this faith in Christ is denial of self. *[437]* One of the few English words of Latin origin (as distinct from those of Anglo-Saxon origin) to be found in the seventeenth century writings is "mortification."[3] To our ears, "mortification" has an antiquarian ring, although the term is still used in some theologies. One dictionary defines it as an "attempt to subordinate the passions and the appetites to the spirit through fasting, penance, abstinence . . . ."[4]

"The term 'asceticism' (Gk *askesis*) originally meant 'practice,' especially the training of an athlete."[5] It no longer involves the kind of "violent penances" of an earlier era that we tend to associate with the word "asceticism." It is a mark of the great differences in modern approaches to asceticism that it can be said that prayer itself can be excellent mortification. It is also typical of modern approaches that they must first of all be psychologically sound and capable of application to everyone even "in an age of 'neurosis.'" St. Theresa of Lisieux "has shown ordinary folk . . . a way of heroism in little things which is within the reach of all."[6]

Reinhold Seeberg pinpointed the essence of asceticism when he stated that it is "self-discipline to make one fit for good works."[7] And Barclay indicates that some of his fellow Christians had some success at this. Among them were many in whom God had "effectively produced a moritification and abstraction from the love and pursuits of this world . . . . Even though they have daily commerce with the world, are married and lawfully employed, this redemption has been as complete as that which used to be considered possible only for those who were cloistered or in monasteries." [394] 8

Fit for Good Works

Fox admonishes Friends "to stand as Nazirites, consecrated to God."9 "Excel the world in . . . humility." Observe that humility which Christ teaches.10 Don't merely "talk of the Lord's words, but practice them," and "be obedient to what he commands and requires."11 Those who "preach Christ, Christ, and do not his will" are found too frequently. There are "too many talkers and few walkers in Christ."12 In "the Power of God, the Gospel . . . there shall be unity" between "words and . . . lives."13

Fox's protest "against keeping feasting, fasting, and praying days" or "observing days, months, times, years" was part of his general caveat against ritualization and calendarization. Christ is the Substance of the types, figures, and shadows that are found in the Old Testament,14 and "you should not fast to make your voice known on high." God knows your needs already.15 "Fast to humble yourselves and not for strife and debate"; that "your health may grow and your light shine."16

Fox sometimes used "fasting" figuratively; exhorting people to keep the Lord's fast, "to fast from sin and iniquity, from strife and debate, from violence and oppression; and to abstain from every appearance of evil." This hortatory advice is based on Isaiah 58, which the *Good News Bible* heads "True Fasting." The passage reads, "The kind of fasting I want is this: Remove the chains of oppression and the yoke of injustice, and let the oppressed go free. Share your food with the hungry and open your homes . . . . Give clothes to those who have nothing to wear . . . ." (Isa. 58:6-7 TEV)

Fox was not against literal fasting on a personal basis where, when undertaken in humility, it could heighten judgment and increase spiritual sensitivity. When James Milner and Richard Myers "went out into imaginations" for a time in 1653 and were followed by others, Fox relates that he kept "a fast about ten days, my spirit being greatly exercised on Truth's account." Within a short time Milner and Myers sent for Fox. He records that they "came to see their folly" and were reconciled, and later Myers' lame arm was spiritually healed through Fox.17 In the previous year Richard Hubberthorne had similarly undergone a long fast. The number of days of fasting is not stipulated, but

Fox records that Hubberthorn was so weak that "people thought he was dead," although to everyone's surprise he recovered rather rapidly.[18]

In the many imprisonments from which over 400 Friends died, mainly because of the horribly unsanitary conditions, there was much time for "solitude." William Penn wrote his *No Cross, No Crown* while in the Tower of London in 1669. *Some Fruits of Solitude* was written in the enforced leisure required by his being deprived of the governorship of Pennsylvania in 1692. Penn's Preface to that work calls solitude "a school few care to learn in," yet, he adds, "until we are persuaded to stop, and step a little aside – out of the noisy crowd, and incumbering hurry of the world – and calmly take a prospect of things, it will be impossible we should be able to make a right judgment . . . ."[19]

In *No Cross, No Crown* Penn says that he would not like to "be thought to slight a true retirement: for I do not only acknowledge but admire solitude. Christ Himself was an example of it: He loved and chose to frequent mountains, gardens, and seasides. It is requisite to the growth of piety, and I reverence the virtue that seeks and uses it . . . I have long thought it an error among all sorts that use not monastic lives, that they have no retreats – for the afflicted, the tempted, the solitary, and the devout – where they might undisturbedly wait upon God; pass through their religious exercises, and, being thereby strengthened, may, with more power over their own spirits, enter into the business of the world again."[20]

The Place of Prayer

It is a pity that Fox and Penn seem to have written very little on the nature of prayer. Most of the statements that they do make are simply warnings against praying without the inspiration of the Spirit. For example, Penn says that whenever prayer is uttered "without the preparation of the Holy Spirit, it is not acceptable with God: nor can it be the true evangelical worship, which is in Spirit and Truth."[21]

Fox, Penn, and Penington have each left at least one printed prayer. Some of these still inspire. Barclay's *Apology* concludes with a prayer, and prayers are scattered throughout William Penn's works. It must have been a great experience to hear them pray publicly. We know that this was true of Fox, for Penn's memorial to him states that "it was precisely in prayer that Fox excelled." He adds that the most awe-filled "living, reverent frame I ever felt or beheld . . . was his in prayer. He knew and lived nearer to the Lord than other men."[22]

It should be stressed that although the early Friends sometimes separated various aspects of life or belief in order to analyze them in some detail—just as we have done here—they were not separated for long. Disassociating them is something like analyzing music by its individual chords, or describing the colors in a butterfly's wings one by one. Under normal circumstances faith and individual discipline, worship and works, were all kept closely together. This was particularly true of Fox. In his writings one aspect of these flows almost imperceptibly into another, and then back again.

In discussing Christ (as the page references to the *Apology* that follow indicate) Barclay has made some separation to facilitate discussion. But I do him no injustice or any violence to his theology in combining the following affirmations. Christ, he says, is not only "the Author of the Christian religion," *[263]* but he is the "Author of works," *[151, 153]* as well.

"Works proceed naturally from . . . Spiritual rebirth and the inward formation of Christ." *[134]* "The chief purpose of all religion is to redeem men . . . and to lead them into inward communion with God . . . . All vain and empty customs . . . which divert the mind from the witness of God in the heart, should be given up . . . Christians should have a living sense of reverence for God, and should be leavened with the evangelical Spirit, which leads into sobriety, gravity, and Godly fear." *[389]*

It was the insistence that both holiness and service on behalf of fellow Christians (and others as well) were equally obligatory upon every true believer that gave unique shape to the early Quaker vision. The inseparability and inescapability of these aspects of faith led to a conviction that without steadfast righteousness and obedience the church in that locale not only becomes "invisible," it ceases to exist in any real sense. Where holiness and service prevail together, some of the results are a unique approach to worship, to personal redemption, and to the way in which both Church and society are to be ordered.

> "Even so, come Lord Jesus!
> More and more set up your Kingdom
> in the souls of the children of men;
> that the holy will of your Fatther
> may be done on earth;
> that mercy and truth,
> righteousness and peace,
> may kiss each other.

> So shall the kingdoms of this world
> become the Kingdoms of the Lord,
> and of his Christ;
> who is God over all,
> blessed forever."[23]

Notes to Chapter 9

Italic figures in brackets within the text refer to page numbers in *Barclay's Apology in Modern English.*

1. The particular reference here is to his Response (pp. 45-46) to the Comments on the abridgement, which appeared in *Quaker Religious Thought* 18:1 (Autumn 1978): 4-34 of Chapter 5, "Early Quaker Ecclesiology," from his *Grace and Faith: The Means to Salvation* (Pittsburgh, 1975), Catholic and Quaker Study #3 (available from C. & Q.S., 1110 Wildwood Ave., Manasquan, NJ 08736. $7.50 plus $1.25 postage and handling).
2. Cf. the present author's "Not a Steeple, a Steeple, a Steeple," *The Friends Quarterly* 18:8 (October 1974): 377-382, in the special issue published on the 350th anniversary of Fox's birth.
3. "Mortification" was probably allowed because the verb form does occur twice in the King James Version of the Bible, suggesting that it was not philosophical in derivation. Perhaps the word "mortification" was used in order to avoid the overtones of murder and violence which accompany *thanatoō* and *nekroō* when they are translated as "putting to death" in some modern translations of Romans 8:13 and Colossians 3:5. These connotations seem hard to escape, even though the "death" referred to is a spiritual one—that is, the demise of our "lower natures."
4. The dictionary referred to is Donald T. Kauffman, *The Dictionary of Religious Terms* (Westwood, NJ: Revell, 1967), p. 319.
   The hair shirt, chains, and other forms of mild physical abuse that were once characteristic are no longer a part of Christian penitential procedures.
5. *The New Schaff-Herzog Encyclopedia of Religious Knowledge*, Samuel Macauley Jackson, Editor-in-Chief (New York: Funk and Wagnalls, 1908), s.v. "asceticism," vol. 1, p. 309.
6. Dom Ralph Russell, O.S.B., s.v. "asceticism," in *A Catholic Dictionary of Theology* (London: Nelson, 1962), vol. 1, pp. 166-168.
7. *New Schaff-Herzog, loc. cit.*, 311b.
8. William Penn uses somewhat similar terms: "The Christian convent and monastery are within, where the soul is encloistered from sin. And this religious house the true followers of Christ carry about with them, who exempt not themselves from the conversation [i.e., activities] of the world, though they keep themselves from the evil of the world in their conversation." *No Cross, No Crown*, c.5, s. 11, p. 62.
9. George Fox, *Journal*, revised edition by John L. Nickalls (Cambridge: University Press, 1952), p. 680.
10. George Fox, *Journal*, Bi-Centenary edition (London, 1891), II:489, 420.
11. Fox, *Journal*, Nickalls, p. 144. George Fox, *Works of George Fox*, 8 vols. (Philadelphia: M.T.C. Gould, 1831) 8:122.
12. Fox, *Works of George Fox*, 8:139, 155. Cf. also, 4:43, 6:174, 7:33. Fox, *Journal*, Bi-Centenary edition, II:244.
13. Fox, *Works of George Fox*, 4:187.
14. Fox, Manuscript source, Aa 25, 10F. 132 and Fox, *Journal*, Bi-Centenary edition, II:367.
15. Fox, *Works of George Fox*, 4:111, 112.
16. Fox, Manuscript source, Aa 39A, p. 51 and Fox, *Works of George Fox*, 7:156.
17. Fox, *Journal*, Nickalls, p. 147.

18 *Ibid.*, 142.
19 Wm. Penn, *Works*, (London: Phillips, 1825) III, pp. 351, 352.
20 Wm. Penn, *No Cross, No Crown*, C. 5, s. 14, pp. 65-66.
21 *Ibid.*, C. 6, s. 3, p. 69.
22 Cf. Dean Freiday, "George Fox (1624-1691)," No. 5 in a series on Post-Reformation Spirituality, in the British Jesuit journal, *The Month*, 237:1301 (February 1976): 59.
23 From William Penn's "A Reply to a . . . Nameless Author" (1695) in Wm. Penn, *Works*, III, p. 350.
    The only changes made were in the punctuation, and the "updating" of two words: the use of "your" for "thy"; and substitution of "on earth" for "in earth."

Chapter 10
BOTTOM-LINE CHRISTIANITY*

Reference has already been made to Father Nesti's thesis. In it he spells out first-generation Quakerism's understanding of "what it meant to be obedient, in the most profound scriptural meaning of the word . . . . This ministry of corporate obedience was founded on Christ who was acting in and through each person in the meeting . . . ." That kind of obedient response required "a God-given belief that something of the divine resides in and works through every person no matter how repugnant that person may seem."[1] Churches collectively are as equally accountable as the component individuals for faithful and righteous obedience. Either you and your meeting/church *are* or you are *not* worthy of the name of your Master.

In addition to this authenticity requirement, both continuity and immediacy are called for. Faith cannot be put in escrow until the time for application may seem more appropriate. Now is the time, "for the days are evil (Eph. 5:16) and yours are but very few."[2] Use your time wisely and well and in well-doing. This call to righteousness is another way of saying that you cannot expect good fruits from evil lives. Or, as Scripture puts it, you must cease doing evil before you can learn to do good (Isa. 1:16-17).[3]

A further guard against postponing the application of faith was found in the Old Testament prophetic imagery of a Day of Visitation. In that Day God's grace seeks out every person for an

---

Defined as: "Being of some earthly good to somebody."

unknown and indeterminable time. But once the Day of Visitation has expired, the possibility of redemption is forever lost, and there is no court of appeal in heaven or on earth.

These truths exist between the lines of Barclay's *Apology* and in the writings of Fox and Penn. Although most of them are not developed systematically, they become apparent when the writings of all three are viewed together. Barclay gives a very good and thoroughly documented presentation of what later generations have called the "Testimonies." Penn's *No Cross, No Crown*, on the other hand, is a prolonged examination of the role of self-denial and spiritual preparation. Fox in turn deals explicitly with the place of fasting, and above all, the constructive value of suffering.

In addition, Fox's unique conceptions of Gospel Order, Unity with the Creation, the centrality of *koinonia* in all interrelationships; and of Christ as Model, as Governor, as Inspirer, as Teacher and Prophet – and His relevance in a hundred other ways – not only make solid the Foundation but buttress every aspect of Christian living. For early Friends, Christ was not only the *object* of faith, but the *method* of achieving it, and the *model* for its practice. In their view, we are and can do "nothing without Christ." *[286]*

The Church

In an earlier chapter it was pointed out that by adopting the categories of "visible church" and "invisible church," which originated in the third century with the Alexandrians, Clement and Origen, and which were in favor with his Protestant contemporaries, Barclay distorted the view of ecclesiology found in Fox. Fr. Nesti has stated that by and large the early Friends did not conceive of the Church "as being composed of a visible aspect. Theirs was an attempt at a totally spiritual ecclesiology based on individual experience of the internal witness of the Spirit. Anyone who had experienced the interior call of God to salvation and had responded to that call in faith was a member of the Church . . . . This did not mean, however, that those who were members of the Church through faith could not or would not recognize each other and be drawn together into a corporate witness of fellowship and holiness."

"This differed greatly from saying that certain structures, rites, creeds, etc. . . . are constituent elements of the unity among believers . . . . Any structures attached to the corporate fellowship of the Church were purely secondary and non-essential .... Men could see that the Spirit was working in the true Church by its lived unity and the fact that its members lived holy lives."[4]

"The Quakers never denied that the Church had a corporate aspect," but in no sense was it "visible" because of its structure. They distinguished "between structural visibility and the visibility of corporate witness."[5] "Structures and organization were only for serving the needs of those already reconciled and united to God through his light."[6] The Church was a "spiritual household" built of "living stones." (1 Pet. 2:5)[7]

In this view, men cannot "construct a Church. God alone gathers a people to himself, because this gathering into God and into Christ consists in one's experience of being transformed and saved in the grace of Christ."[8] "Every action is now God-directed." And it is "this experience of the total redirection of ... personality [that] is the cause of ... joy, hope, and general confidence in being able to do what God wills."[9]

Fellowship "is not achieved simply by saying that one is in the Spirit. Instead it is a fellowship with Christ in his sufferings and death as well as his resurrection. It is a fellowship which calls for a renunciation of self and living for God alone .... The effect of this ... can only be one of *peace* – personal and corporate as well. The *liberty* allowed in the *non-essentials* leads to a deep *tolerance* of the rights of others and not to the limited fallible judgments of a few. There is no contention to be found in true spiritual unity. 'God is not the author of confusion, but of peace'" (1 Cor. 14:33)[10]

"The actual holiness of Quaker life verified their claim to be the true Church. They were so closely united to Christ in thought, word, and action that they were to be recognized as the body of Christ present to the world."[11] Although Fr. Nesti considered this theory of the Church in need of some modification when the facts are considered empirically as they relate to the latter part of the seventeenth century, he does not bring into question the holiness of those Friends. His modification concerns "mediation" (as he sees it) and entails some "structural visibility" as a "sign" of the presence of the Kingdom. Whether the ministry to which he refers should be considered "mediation" or be construed merely as "facilitating" grace is a fine point that need not be dealt with here.

Quakerism today unquestionably has a bureaucracy. But it operates in a flexible structure that still responds to any serious inquiry by anyone, and it is a unique partnership between staff and nonsalaried appointees. It is a *koinonia* in which Gospel Order prevails. All are subordinated only to a heavenly Master, whose living Presence governs all decisions. No appointment confers any arbitrary authority. There are no majority votes. And there are few heated arguments.

Self-discipline is necessary in this, as in all aspects of Quaker life and worship. Peace and unity are its hallmarks, and any "sign" value would seem to attach to whether or not these "marks" of holiness prevail and indicate that a heavenly Source of Wisdom has been heeded.[12]

There are enough examples of modern departure from seventeenth century practice to support the thesis that it is detrimental to admit any form of sacralization other than holiness of life and conduct. "Meeting houses" soon become "sanctuaries." Bureaucracies are on their way toward institutionalization. Pastors tend to become "clergy," and ministry in general is on its way toward professionalization and monopolization. Any claim to being a reliving of first century Christian experience develops ambiguity and becomes open to the charge of "apostasy" – the very charge that early Friends so frequently leveled at others.

Behavioral Guidelines

Father Nesti has been quoted to the effect that it "is far from easy to live and sustain" the holiness of life that early Quakers considered essential, and the precondition (if not in time at least in nature) for all Christian witness and work. "Relationships" of *this quality*, he said, "require a highly developed asceticism." It might be added that when this emphasis upon righteousness or holiness is coupled with reluctance to harden beliefs into creed or dogma, it becomes even more difficult to sustain such relationships. This is particularly true when the lives are to be lived out "in the world" and not under the discipline of cloister or cell.

The demands of an everchanging existence, which no behavioral code, however carefully worked out, could anticipate, were formulated through a doctrine of continuing revelation. Christ had come again (in the Spirit) to teach His people Himself. And He would guide them into ever-new areas of witness and service, or show them the way forward in ongoing commitments. What He would teach "in the Spirit" would be consistent with what He taught when He "became flesh." But this kind of interpretation of Scripture – by the ongoing Light given by Christ's Spirit – can lead to neither formalism nor codification.[13]

What this resistance to formalism and codification did lead to was a set of customary practices and certain responses to the culture. The way in which one witnessed for Christ in daily life was called "Testimony." In time Testimony came to be broken up into "Testimonies," each governing behavior in a particular social situation or in a particular political or cultural context. John McCandless has correctly pointed out that the early Friends asserted that Christian righteousness is not properly the product of rational insights. It is neither "a code of behavior" nor "a social and political program" but "a response to the lordship, oversight, and prophetic teaching Voice of Jesus Christ."

It is difficult, he continues, to avoid a programmatic approach, an agenda for social change. Testimony easily becomes a series of "testimonies" representing positions on particular issues. "As testimony becomes merely a position . . . something that the individual, or the local group, can accept or reject," it becomes easy to "water it down." It has lost the immediacy of "personal relationship and application to Christ's guidance." It also becomes easier "as our understanding of 'Testimony' loses its personal reference, to add new positions that are picked up" from either a liberal or a conservative agenda.[14]

Living in the Presence and the Power

William Penn states that in the first Christian community "where once nothing was examined" about their daily practices, after the Apostles followed Christ "nothing went unexamined." A strict guard was "kept upon the very wicket of the soul." Now, not only every deed, but "every thought must come to judgment and the rise and tendency of it" must be approved. Early Christian lives were conspicuous for the daily "self-denial" and the "integrity" that "dwelt with Christians." And "mighty was the Presence, and invincible that Power that attended them."[15]

The early Quakers, whose lives seemed to repeat the experience of the Apostles and the first century Church in so many ways, had a similar experience. Penn says that in mortification—that is, the dying of the old Adam—"a grand inquest came upon our whole life: every word, thought, and deed was brought to judgment, the root examined and its tendency considered."[16] What followed this examination was far from a lapse into mere pietism, for "true godliness does not turn men out of the world, but enables them to live better in it, and excites their endeavors to mend it."[17] Penn encapsulates the Gospel in six words, and thus reiterates what he means: "believe, receive, and apply Him [Christ] rightly."[18]

Before Quakers could take positive steps to "mend" the world, they found it necessary to be negative and reject a few of its practices. Most of these their contemporaries took for granted; or else they considered them God-given, or the marks of good breeding. The best organized report of what these things were is found in the final chapter of Barclay's *Apology*, and it is not necessary to catalogue them here. It seems more desirable to find some of the common denominators and the positive aspects of their witness that could serve as a basis for their application to our own situation.

Verbal Accountability

In refusing oaths, rejecting honorifics and the empty or stilted salutations and so-called "polite forms" used both in correspondence and speech, at least five cardinal principles interacted.

Truth. The first of these was an extraordinarily high standard of truth. Scripture is complex in its handling of this subject. There is no specific word for "truth" in the Old Testament, although "faith" carries some of its overtones. In Hebrew "faith-truth" is not something for mere intellectual assent, but a matter that requires personal commitment. In some passages of the New Testament "true" means the "real" or what is authentic; in others it stands for "truthfulness" or "sincerity" (in a way that is commensurate with our ordinary usage). In the Pauline literature "truth" often stands in opposition to unrighteousness, or it is used in parallel to righteousness. And in Johannine (and some other literature) God and God alone is Truth. Or Truth can symbolize the fact that our knowledge of God is limited, and then Truth represents what we do know of God—"the divinely revealed reality of God manifested in the words and the person of Jesus Christ."[19]

Accountability. Some seldom-noticed words of Jesus provided a second cardinal principle, accountability. Matthew 12:36 is cited both by Penn[20] and by Barclay. *[409]* In that passage Christ warns that on Judgment Day we will not only have to account for our words, but also answer for "every idle word." (KJV) There are few places where Bible translation varies as much as it does for the adjective that is used here. There is reference to these words being "unfounded" (JerB), "unguarded" (NAB), "thoughtless" (Knox and NEB), "careless" (Goodspeed, RSV, NIV, NASB), or "foolish" (Lamsa). But, whichever nuance is selected, there is a clear injunction to have the highest regard for Truth and to be precise in speech.

Precision in speech was something Friends observed meticulously until perhaps 25 years ago. But although there seems to be some diminution in the exactness of conversational speech, carefully worded minutes and printed statements continue to exhibit a preciseness that almost constitutes a fetish. This precision resulted not only from concepts of Truth and Accountability, but also from a reaction to what we label today as stereotyping.

Stereotyping. The word *stereotyping* did not come into figurative use in English until the beginning of the nineteenth century; and in recent years it has been redeployed as a broader and slightly less pejorative (but nearly synonymous) replacement for the term "caricature." The only figurative meaning the *Oxford English Dictionary* (1933) gives for stereotyping is "to fix or perpetuate in an unchanging form." Apparently there is no antonym. In our time, any black, or any victim of sexist discrimination is well aware of the "perpetuating" role of language. The use of certain words limits the victim's behavior by constantly slotting that person in an inferior role.

Whether or not committing verbal androcide by deleting all references to maleness is the correct route to equal and just opportunities for women, the attempts at rewording to avoid "sexist language" certainly put the spotlight on the role of language in shaping social structure. To refer to a mature man as a "boy" or to use some other patronizing or degrading appellation is not as complete a depersonalization as selling him at auction, but the serious breach of his human dignity is bound to have devaluing side effects and to make for a gradual deterioration in human sensitivity on the part of the person who indulges in such practices.

The early Friends were very conscious of the "perpetuating" role of language in a somewhat broader sense—the reinforcement of class or caste by the use (often unconscious) of role-graded language. Power and privileged behavior could be perpetuated (and persons restricted to inferior roles) by the use of certain types of customary language. "Superiors" were addressed as "you." Equals or inferiors as "thou." Hats were doffed and bows were made before their "majesties," or even their "honors," their "reverences," or their "lordships." Subtler distinctions were made between "stations" and "places" in life. In our own era, such shades of meaning continue between "wages, salaries, professional fees, and honoraria." One does not give a plumber or a butcher an "honorarium," even though the amount paid may be considerably greater.

In Christian eyes God is no respecter of persons, but this did not mean the abolition of "station" or "wealth" for the early Friends. It did mean greater responsibility for those more favored. They were no "levellers," although a social movement among their contemporaries bore that designation. While different roles in some particulars seemed more suitable for women and children – resulting in separate but equal business meetings for women then, and continuing for young people now (as in a junior yearly meeting) – age and sex made no difference in the spoken ministry. Women as well as men traveled two-by-two in the ministry in peacetime years to Europe, America, and even the Near East. To cite a more recent example, it was a Junior Yearly Meeting minute addressed to New York Yearly Meeting, asking that the adults not prolong differences that were meaningless to youth, that finally brought about the uniting of two formerly separate yearly meetings.

Truth also played a role along with rejection of stereotypes in the early Quaker disuse of honorifics and stilted pleasantries. They recognized that inheriting a title does not necessarily entail inheriting the qualities that marked its first bearer. They were aware of the fact that to ascribe "honor" or "reverence" where none exists represents a shading and consequent devaluation of truth. The positive side of this attitude was that a deliberate setting out to shatter stereotypes not only liberates both the stereotyper and stereotypee but it can revalue properly their common situation under God. The spiritual growth that this fostered is evident in the serving maids and tradesmen among the early Friends whose gifts in the ministry have been recorded for all time alongside those of an Admiral's son (Penn) and the son of the Puritan Lord Mayor of London (Penington).

The Magna Carta for this solicitude for the dignity of all was Gal. 3:28: *[218]* "There are no more distinctions between Jew and Greek, slave and free, male and female, but all of you are one in Christ Jesus." (JerB) This changed situation brought about by faith is alluded to elsewhere by Paul (Rom. 10:12; 1 Cor. 12-13), and it has its basis in renewal in the Image of the Creator in Col. 3:11: "In that image there is no room for distinction . . . . There is only Christ: he is everything and he is in everything." (JerB)

God is One. If we are to be renewed in the Image of God, we will do well to recall God's oneness, not simply that He is the *only* God but that He is *unity*. Although Fox was a "Hebrew thinker" – more at home in Old Testament ways of thinking than in the arid intellectualism of Greek philosophy – he approached unity indirectly. For him it was something given by the Holy Spirit. But for the devout Jew who recites the Shema, the central prayer that begins with Deut. 6:4-9, God himself is "Unity." The prayer starts: "Hear, O Israel; The Lord our God is One Lord."

We hear much today about "holistic" approaches. The Shema is prototypical of these. God's "oneness" is His "wholeness" and consistency. It is also His "holiness." This in turn is required of His worshipers. "One" is also an "integer," and the latter word is the etymological source of "integrity." The synonym for integrity, "one-mindedness" (unlike duplicity or equivocation) also equates with "simplicity," which is the avoidance of superfluity or extravagance in honor of the God whose own simplicity means that He "is a most pure and un-complicated being, devoid of all composition or division." (Barclay's statement here, /85/ be it noted, is good Roman Catholic doctrine.) In one-mindedness the Christian shuns evil or unjust practices, so once more holiness and wholeness come to the fore.

Thus it is from the Oneness or Simplicity of God that the ideals of unity, integrity, and humility stem. They assume great importance for Life in Christ. When Christ set forth the two great commandments (Mt. 22:36-40), the first of these – loving God with all one's heart, and soul, and mind – is derived from the later verses of the Shema. Its complement, of course, was love of neighbor of the same kind one would want applied to oneself.

Consistency. Consistency was another cardinal principle that applied to deeds as well as speech. Consistency requires the application of the same principles in all situations. One does not behave in one way in business and in another way in educational or political situations. Nor is one only as ethical as the situation requires. Nor does one apply one standard to one person, another to a second, and still another to a third. Truth is truth, however puzzled Pilate was and we may be as to its precise nature. But as far as we can discern its demands, we are to follow them wherever we go, whatever we do.

Living "in the Kingdom" could begin now, in early Quaker eyes. Christ left us sufficient teaching about the governing qualities of the reign of God to enable us to apply them, however imperfect the present synthesis might be. And with His living Presence as a guide, ever new vistas of their meaning and their application in our situation would continue to open up.

Accountability for Time

Time is a complex subject in Fox's theology. Today we speak of *kairos*, meaning appropriate time; and *kronos*, meaning chronological time. We also speak of eschatology—meaning the final times or End time. Curiously, Fox often reads as though he were aware of these subtleties. The Day of the Lord symbolizes the final time—which brings all of God's purposes to a focus, and to Judgment. The Day of Visitation symbolizes the fact that God's Grace and Mercy are not extended to the individual forever.

Fox also has a very clear sense of "eternity." It is *not* something that goes on and on in chronological terms. It *is* something that existed before "time," will extend beyond "time," and indeed is exempt from "time." It is closely related to what is meant by the more philosophical term "transcendence." It is also a quality. Eternal life can be experienced now as it breaks into our humdrum existence.

All of these ideas come to bear in Fox's handling of "time." *Now* is the appropriate time to act, "when the wicked's sun is gone down, their day is ended . . . and then the people-of-God's day approaches."[21] Time also relates to sufferings, for Fox admonishes, with reference to "the rod of the wicked" or Psa. 125:3, that it will not be long. "Never heed prisons, for they are but for a time . . . Mind Him that hath all times and seasons in His hand." (Wis. 7:16-18)[22] Chronologically, for Fox, history is a series of "times": there was "the state and time before the Law, the time of the Law, the time of Christians, and the time of the apostasy."[23]

"Christ," however, "is Son of God before Abraham was, before Jerusalem was." He it was "who came out of time—from God—into time," and "who fetches up out of time to where there is no time."[24] "God hath spoken to us by his Son in these last times" (Heb. 1:2), and "no time is beyond God the Father and his Son's time, for he is first and last." (Rev. 22:13)[25] "All the figures and shadows were and are comprehended in time, but Christ the Substance is the Beginning and the Ending."[26]

"Be heirs and possessors of Christ and his government . . . of the increase of this heavenly man's government there is no end." (Isa. 9:7)[27] If you "are in Him," you "will not be weary nor faint, nor think the time long of your sufferings," for such thoughts "are in Adam in the Fall."[28] Instead, you will wear "the breastplate of righteousness," which will save and protect "your hearts and minds."[29]

"Actions done in time" when brought to "the eternal Light" will be "condemned and confounded" if they are "out of plainness."[30] And those that are of a contrary nature to the Light will have to be "given an account of . . . in the Day of Judgment,"[31] for then both "the wicked and the righteous . . . shall have their wages." For all "must have their time, their work, and their day; and in the End their wages."[32] Therefore, "prize your time while you have it, that you spend it to the honor and glory of God."[33]

Thus accountability for time like that for words should influence one's commitments. Barclay cites 1 Cor. 7:29-35, where Paul reminds the Corinthians that "'the time is short' and that they should make the most of it." He also cites the advice of 1 Pet. 1:17 (NEB) to "stand in awe of him" while you "live out your time on earth." *[408]*[34] Penn also asks: "Had you the Spirit of Christianity indeed, could you consume your most precious little time in so many unnecessary visits, games, and pastimes; in your vain compliments, courtships, feigned stories, flatteries, and fruitless novelties, and what not?"[35]

There should be no "idle talking, no vain jesting, but . . . meditating all the day long."[36] Penn tells people that they should learn "to number their days that they may not be surprised with their dissolution; and to redeem their time, because the days are evil." (Eph. 5:16)[37] The early Quaker journals were not merely spiritual diaries, as we are apt to think of them, but they were also books of account, a sort of advance audit of how wisely and well they had spent their time.

Penn charges that not only did a typical fellow Christian "omit to take up Christ's holy yoke, to bear thy daily cross"; but "thou wast careless of thy affections, and kept no journal or check upon thy actions; but didst decline to audit accounts in thy own conscience, with Christ thy Light, the great Bishop of thy soul and Judge of thy works."[38]

These Gospel times . . . are the proper times for the effusion of the Spirit as prophesied by Joel and noted in Acts (Joel 2:28; Acts 2:17). The miracles and wonders that will precede "the great and glorious Day of the Lord" are described in the later verses there. They conclude, "Then, whoever calls out to the Lord for help will be saved." (Acts 2:19-21 TEV) Penn's advice is: "'Walk circumspectly, not as fools, but as wise, redeeming the time, because the days are evil.'" (Eph. 5:15-16)[39]

Notes to Chapter 10

Italic figures in brackets within the text refer to page numbers in *Barclay's Apology in Modern English*.

1. The material here is taken from Donald S. Nesti, C.S.Sp., "Early Quaker Ecclesiology," *Quaker Religious Thought*, vol. 18, no. 1 (Autumn 1978) :4-34. The article is a slightly abridged version of Chapter 5 (bearing the same title) of Fr. Nesti's *Grace and Faith: The Means to Salvation* (Pittsburgh, 1975). It is Catholic and Quaker Study #3, 368 pp., available from C. & Q. S., 1110 Wildwood Ave., Manasquan, NJ 08736. $7.50 plus $1.25 postage and handling.

    The quoted portion is from Donald Nesti's "Response" to Comments in the *QRT* issue cited, pp. 45-46.
2. William Penn, *No Cross, No Crown*, c. 18, s. 11, p. 286.
3. Robert Barclay, *Apology*, p. 279. Also Wm. Penn, *No Cross, No Crown*, c. 6, s. 9, p. 77, reads: "Cease to do evil, learn to do well."
4. Nesti, *Quaker Religious Thought* 18:1 (Aut. '78): 33-34.
5. *Ibid.*, p. 7.
6. *Ibid.*, p. 9.
7. *Ibid.*, p. 10.
8. *Ibid.*, p. 11.
9. *Ibid.*, p. 19.
10. *Ibid.*, p. 19. Italics in original.
11. *Ibid.*, p. 23.
12. Fox develops a strong contrast between fallible human wisdom and the Wisdom that is from God. The dependence here, as in any aspect of structure or procedure whether for business or worship, is not upon professionalism but prophetism. Even "know-how," recognized as "weightiness," is applied under the direct guidance of Christ. It is He who presides, and who makes His will known to those who have spiritual "ears to hear." Mt. 11:15)
13. See Dean Freiday, "The Early Quakers and the Doctrine of Authority," *Quaker Religious Thought* 15:1 (Aut. '73): 4-38, especially pp. 36-38.
14. J. H. McCandless, "Thoughts on Righteousness," *New Foundation Papers* #6 (Nov. '81): 4, 6.
15. Penn, *No Cross, No Crown*, c. 2, ss. 6 & 7, pp. 22 & 23
16. *Ibid.*, c. 9, s. 6, p. 119.
17. *Ibid.*, c. 5, s. 12, p. 63.
18. *Ibid.*, c. 2, s. 4, p. 17.
19. John L. McKenzie, S.J. *Dictionary of the Bible* (Milwaukee: Bruce, 1965), s. v. "Truth," pp. 901-902.
20. Penn, *No Cross, No Crown*, c. 6, s. 1, p. 68.
21. George Fox, *Works of George Fox*, 8 vols. (Philadelphia: M.T.C. Gould, 1831) 7:239.
22. *Ibid.*, 7:258.
23. *Ibid.*, 7:263.
24. Fox, Manuscript source, 21 (19, 67A).
25. *Ibid.*, V 22 (10, 50F).
26. George Fox, *Journal*, Bi-Centenary edition (London, 1891), II:418.
27. Fox, *Works of George Fox*, 8:51.
28. *Ibid.*, 7:257-258.
29. *Ibid.*, 7:203.
30. *Ibid.*, 7:112.
31. Fox, Manuscript source, aa 74 (123 C).
32. *Ibid.*, V 50 (5, 29E).
33. Fox, *Works of George Fox*, 8:299.
34. Penn, *op. cit.*, c. 9, s. 34, p. 143.
35. *Ibid.*, c. 10, s. 9, p. 160.
36. *Ibid.*, c. 16, s. 1, p. 245.
37. *Ibid.*, c. 4, s. 23, p. 51.
38. *Ibid.*, c. 2, s. 8, p. 25.
39. *Ibid.*, c. 15, s. 3, p. 232.

Appendix 1

Catholicity and Quakerism

"Catholicity" may seem a strange note to bring into a discussion of Quaker theology, but it can serve to evaluate several aspects of faith. The renewal movement within Quakerism launched by Lewis Benson and now fostered by New Foundations began with his study of *Catholic Quakerism*, proclaiming that Friends were not just a Peace Church or a social-action group, but a vital form of Christianity.[1] Catholicity reminds us that narrow concentration on one belief (almost to the point of excluding others) becomes idolatrous, and it is the mark of a sect – something less than the fullness of the Christian Gospel.

In spite of some regressive tendencies, Quakers seem to be moving beyond the era when one group of Friends could be distinguished from the other by whether it spoke of the "Inner Light" or about "Christ within." Catholicity (as well as anything that could be called faithfulness to our beginnings) requires us to proclaim the inward work of Christ and to keep this in close relation to what we know of His earthly history from Scripture. If Christ never lived, He can hardly be spoken of as the "living Christ" who becomes present in the midst of His faithful people in all ages.

Sooner or later, some limits will have to be set on what can be rightfully called "Quaker." However, we need first to look objectively at varieties other than our own. If partisanship can be avoided, and we leave it to Christ to teach His people Himself, He will separate what is spurious from what is Truth. What is more, He will open up new ways of understanding our mission and our goals. When we can develop a single eye toward a common Lord, the Spirit of Christ will bring us into unforeseen unity.

If there is any skepticism about discussing catholicity in a Quaker context, the validity of doing so can be established from our writers. William Penn did not *begin* to describe his faith for a personal friend – Dr. John Tillotson, who a few years later became Archbishop of Canterbury – by discussing catholicity, as much importance as the claim for that mark of the Church has always had for Anglicanism.[2] But when Penn thought he had sufficiently cleared himself of charges that he was an ordained graduate of St. Omer's, a Jesuit who sometimes officiated at Mass in James II's chapel, he declared in a nonpejorative way: "I am a Catholic, though not a Roman."

While to us the charge against Penn seems ridiculous, humorous even, it was no laughing matter in the seventeenth century. Penn's fortunes were seriously affected by it over and over.[3]

In both the broad Christian context, and our own current denominational situation, considerations of catholicity can be quite constructive in providing some perspective on where we are, and where we ought to be. The core meaning of catholicity could be stated as "comprehensiveness."[4] In part, it emphasizes *"inclusiveness with integrity"* – something quite different from an accidental drift into syncretism. Catholicity is also quite *opposite to "sectarianism,"* in the sense of a narrow triumphalist concentration on a few particulars of doctrine or practice, the kind of doctrinal development that might be described as lopsided rather than symmetrical.

It is gratifying to many within the fold that Quakerism seems to be developing a considerable sense of theological responsibility coupled with awareness of the pitfalls of overemphasis or narrowness. Initial moves have been made to enter an era in which practices formerly considered mutually exclusive can be held together creatively. Over a ten-year period, a Faith and Life Panel, with across-the-spectrum representation of the sub-species, shared insights into what is constructively held in common.

In actual practice both "unprogrammed worship" and "programmed worship" can be found not only within the same yearly meeting or association of yearly meetings, but often in the same building and jointly supervised by the same meeting for business. Different forms of worship need not be either competitive or divisive. In actual fact, their coexistence could very well result in a deeper examination of the meaning of worship and a recovery of its correct context, namely a sense of the living Presence of Christ and of being under His direct guidance.

Perhaps a fruitful exchange on the subject of ministry can develop between the monopastoral and shared-ministry varieties. If so, such dialogue might even have a part in deterring the drift of many forms of mainline or electronic ministry into "the unholy trinity" of "professionalism, consumerism, and theatricalism."[5]

At the present time, however, Faith and Order discussions in the ecumenical sphere seem to have returned to a method of "comparative ecclesiology" from the magnificent breakthrough into the "Post-Lund methodology" that had such fruitful effects for Montreal[6] (and to some extent, for Vatican II). Fortunately, this regression is not endemic to all ecumenical efforts be they within or outside the World Council of Churches.

The Roman Catholic Church, a relatively late entrant into ecumenical activities (although preparative studies date back to Pius XII and earlier), has brought new breadth and freshness into such endeavors. Not only do the Decrees and Directories of Vatican II embrace whatever of Christianity exists in other ecclesial communities, the documents and their implementation go even further. There is new regard for persons as human beings, regardless of whether they are persons of faith or not.

The age of heresy is over. One of the effects of the change is that in some respects there is timidity at present about expressing what you stand for – simply because it might seem to have antagonistic connotations. A true ecumenism cannot thrive, however, where differences are swept under the rug or temporarily tabled. Frankness informed by friendliness provides a more realistic basis for permanent rapprochement.

Sharp oppositions have occasionally been drawn in this study, but where these occurred the intent was to clarify with full charity. Catholicity in ecumenical matters necessitates finding ways in which paradoxically opposite concepts of church order, ministry – many things – can live together and reinforce one another, rather than undermine one another as they have so often done in the past.

We serve Christ best when integrity is maintained without antipathy.

Notes to Appendix 1

1 Lewis Benson, *Catholic Quakerism* (publ. by the author, 1966), 87 pp. Reprinted (Philadelphia: Book and Publications Committee of Philadelphia Yearly Meeting, 1968), 115 pp.

2 Cf. George H. Tavard, *The Quest for Catholicity: A Study in Anglicanism* (New York: Herder and Herder, 1964), 237 pp.

3 The whole exchange of letters to and from Tillotson (and a third party) appears in William Penn *Wks.*, v. 1, pp. 67-86 (here p. 69). James II, of course, granted Pennsylvania to Penn in settlement of a debt to Admiral William Penn, his father. James also had a god-fatherly relationship to Penn as a result of a deathbed request that James should "protect me from the inconveniences and troubles my persuasion might expose me to." Penn speaks not only of James's "friendly promise to do it, and exact performances of it" but also tells how James, while Duke of York, had gotten him "out of the Tower of London in 1669" (p. 81). In 1687, at the annual royal audience for dissenters (held to this day) Penn read the message of thanks prepared at the "annual assembly" in London for James's "gracious proclamation and warrants last year, whereby 1200 prisoners were released from their severe imprisonments, and many others from spoil and ruin in their estates and properties." (p. 73) This did not end Penn's troubles. The fact that he was "often at Whitehall," the Royal Residence at that time, was a factor in the suspension of his rights as Governor of Pennsylvania. His friendship with Lord Baltimore probably had a bearing on that action as well. But none of this prevented Penn's stating that it was possible "to be dutiful, thankful, and serviceable to the king, though he be of the Roman Catholic communion." (p. 80)

4 Martin E. Marty has described one of the dimensions of catholicity as: "a quest for wholeness, an all-embracing intent" in his *A Short History of Christianity* (Cleveland: World, 1959) p. 133.

The literal meaning of *katholikos* is "universal," stressing the geographic universality of the Church as opposed to particularity. This is emphasized in the catechisms and creeds. The word also has application to time and doctrine.

Everett F. Harrison (in *Baker's Dict. of Theol.*, 1960, s.v. (under the word) "catholic," states somewhat unapprovingly (p. 112) that catholic is sometimes used "to indicate a breadth of spirit or outlook in contrast to that which is rigidly narrow." He considers this "completely different from the ancient significance."

Donald Attwater (in *A Cath. Dict.*, 1961, s.v. "catholicity," states that "Catholicity is also applied to the teaching of the Church, which embraces the whole deposit of faith and all the necessary means of salvation."

Rahner-Vorgrimler (*Theol. Dict.*, 1965, pp. 68-69) add that "today, catholicity especially signifies an interior, qualitative characteristic of the Church," which, "unlimited by space or time, necessarily stands open to all men . . . and . . . can never be confined to any one culture or race to the exclusion of all others:" possessing as she does "the fullness of God's revelation in Christ."

Curiously *Sacramentum Mundi: An Encyclopedia of Theology* (1968) has no entry under "catholic" or "catholicity"; nor even "marks of the church"! The Thomas Nelson *Cath. Dict. of Theol.*, (1967) (v. 2, p. 5) adds an ecumenical dimension: "Today the real theological meaning of catholicity is seen to be complementary to that of unity. Catholicity suggests multiformity within unity" and not merely "absorption."

Schaff-Herzog Encyc. of Relig. Knowl., (1908, v. 2, p. 457, s.v. "catholic") paraphrases Anglican bishop John Pearson's 1659 *Exposition of the Creed*, art. IX, "as indicating that the Church is to be disseminated through *all* nations, extended to *all* places, and propagated to *all* ages; that it contains in it *all* truths necessary to be known . . . ." (itals. in original).

In spite of Harrison's demurrer, St. Cyril of Jerusalem wrote circa A.D. 350 (*Catech. Lect.* 18, 23) that the Church is called Catholic "because it extends over the whole world . . . teaches universally and infallibly each and every doctrine which must come to the knowledge of men . . . brings every race of men into subjection to godliness . . . and it possesses within itself every conceivable form of virtue, in deeds and in words and in the spiritual gifts of every description." [Wm. A. Jurgens, *Faith of the Early Fathers* (Collegeville, MN: Liturgical Press, 1970), p. 359]

An unsigned *Encyc. Brit.*, 14th ed., article led to the discovery of this concise early statement of the breadth and "comprehensiveness" of catholicity.

5 Cf. my "Response," in *Prayer and Holy Obedience in a War-Wracked World*, papers from a Southern Baptist-Quaker Colloquy, Berea, KY, June 25-27, 1981, ed. by Glenn Igleheart (Atlanta, Ga: Home Mission Board of the Southern Baptist Convention, 1982), p. 29.

6 The Fourth World Conference on Faith and Order of the World Council of Churches in 1963.

Appendix 2

A Discussion of Method, and Some Conclusions

The original intention of this study was to furnish a guide and supplement to the *Apology for the True Christian Divinity* by Robert Barclay (published in Latin in 1676, in English in 1678, and transphrased into modern English by the present writer in 1967). That was my starting point because the years of work in editing, annotating, and transphrasing *Barclay's Apology in Modern English* had been such a personally renewing theological pilgrimage.

Nonetheless, as the work on *Nothing Without Christ* progressed, the conviction soon developed that none of the commonly named theologians of Quakerism's beginning era – George Fox, Robert Barclay, William Penn, Isaac Penington, George Keith, or Samuel Fisher – was equally astute (or comprehensive) in all areas of theology. The longer one works with the writings of George Fox, however, the more one becomes convinced that the depth, originality, and the significance of his thought are sufficiently greater than those of the others to make him normative on most matters. It also becomes clear that he provided the major outlines and the foundations on which they built. And frequently even the way they developed their thought paralleled his, although the terminology in which it was couched might be somehat different.

Indeed, although the theological ferment that Fox initiated was of unusual caliber, and his reexamination of apostolic origins extraordinarily thorough, neither he nor the others exhausted its potentialities. This is true in spite of the fact that Fox's thought was continually refined throughout his life. Next to Fox in general stature is Robert Barclay, who was unquestionably more logical—as opposed to intuitive—and more systematic in organizing his thoughts. Yet Fox's "insights" ("received revelations" would be a less diluted and theologically more congenial term) were more of the order of what we would call "breakthroughs."

Penn had a greater flair than the others for the felicitous phrase. Penington's work possessed a distinctive quality that some have termed "mystical." Others, particularly Keith and Fisher, were unusually perceptive in certain areas; and the general debt of Barclay to Keith is considerable.[1] None of the others possessed the scholarly and technical competence with Scripture demonstrated by Fisher.[2] To acknowledge this in no way minimizes Fox's untutored ability to make subtle and profound use of the Bible. And in spite of the wide acknowledgment of this, adequate research on Fox's use of Scripture is still awaited. However, Douglas Gwyn has developed the Apocalyptic quotient of it in some detail,[3] and a few other aspects have been touched on here.

To return to Robert Barclay, nearly all of the developed portions of his theology are to be found in the *Apology*, except for the treatise on Church government—*The Anarchy of the Ranters*. Other items in his collected works, and a few unpublished essays[4] clarify, enlarge, or defend particular areas of his doctrine, but they add little new ground. Nevertheless, while the *Apology* is the most complete systematic presentation of any of our authors, it is not a *Summa*—an exhaustive treatment.

This is particularly true of aspects of doctrine and practice that do not come within the scope of apologetics, whose particular tasks are defense of the faith and the interpretation of it to the uninitiated. Both tasks require overemphasis upon the unfamiliar—the places where divergences from the doctrine accepted by others are greatest—whereas points commonly shared tend to be treated briefly or taken for granted. This can give the impression that such common elements do not exist, or that the matters left untreated are denied.

An effort was made here to restore balance where necessary, but this study by no means exhausts the riches in the works of these authors. In treating Barclay, even the slightest effort to see his theology whole makes it necessary to emphasize, in particular, that his functional view of the work of Christ was erected on solid beliefs in who the Christ of history was. But if these beliefs are to be readily identified they must be collected and organized from scattered allusions.

It would also be a distortion of Barclay's theology to view his prolonged treatment of the Holy Spirit in isolation, or regard it as in any way unrelated to the Triunity of God.[5] As in the New Testament itself, the emphasis on near-identity of Spirit and the living Christ is so pronounced in Barlcay's work that it leans in the direction of a binitarianism.[6]

However, a binitarianism does not lessen, but heightens, the significance of Christ, although the heightening is at the expense of the Holy Spirit. Grace, Light, Power and other gifts are no longer the "personal" contribution of the Spirit, but the work of the living Christ.

The Light/Grace of the Christ-related Spirit has been developed by Barclay at great length because of the neglect of the experiential and appropriational aspects of Christ by his contemporaries. No other metaphor or title for Christ received as full a treatment, and Barclay can perhaps be charged with over centralization of this aspect. By contrast, although George Fox develops Light/Grace metaphors extensively, he does not neglect *any* of the terms that either Testament uses that are capable of application to Christ. Robert Barclay employs perhaps a dozen of these, and makes no direct mention of "Prophet," which is so important in Fox's christology. Yet Christ is central in significance in Barclay's *a priori* assumptions if not in the explicit development of his theology.

So much, on the other hand, is affirmed by all of our authors that other Christians would not find different, that one needs to remember the "yes, but" points at which their company is parted. For example: "Their notion of God as being beyond the clouds will be of little use to them if they cannot *also* [italics added] find him near them .... Merely talking about the outward life of Christ on earth will not redeem or justify them .... They must know Christ resurrected in them ... [and] sense the presence of God in and near themselves." *[438]*

If there is any dividing line between mainstream thought and that of these writers on many points of doctrine, it is far from obvious. Take such affirmations as: "the Father through the appearance of his beloved son, the Lord Jesus Christ ... did and does deliver us by suffering and dying." *[275]* Or, again, the "Captain of our salvation," *[374]* is none other than the "meek and self-denying Jesus." *[404]* "The Stone rejected ... has become the Cornerstone for us," *[110]* and "we can do nothing without Christ." *[286]*

What was common to all of our authors was primarily the stressing of the interiorizing, appropriation, and application of the functional aspects of Christ's life and works. This was also what distinguished them most from their Christian contemporaries; and these remain aspects of faith that tend to be underdeveloped in much of Protestantism today. Even Catholicism, in spite of the importance of the spiritual and experiential elements in its heritage, has tended to leave such matters to the religious orders while they have diminished in importance for the average Catholic.

Although Quakerism witnesses to the experiential dimensions of Christian life, that witness is handicapped both by the small number of practitioners, and often by the lack of conviction or the articulateness of the advocates. Where fresh currents of spirituality seem to be arising today, as on many other matters of renewal, they appear to be the product of the extreme vitality shown by biblical studies, an area in which particular vigor is being demonstrated by American Catholic scholars. Many of the same truths enunciated by Friends in the seventeenth century are being arrived at quite independently today through Scripture studies; and frequently they are seen with greater clarity and stated with a more compelling quality.

The seventeenth century in England produced so many fundamental advances in a number of fields from science to religion that it sometimes seems that comparatively nothing happened in the eighteenth or nineteenth centuries. We appear to be picking up where the seventeenth century left off. On a historical level, at least, the theological and biblical insights of one small group of Christians of that century deserve much more credit than they have received even among scholars of their own tradition. Some of these were quite willing to be classed historically as left-wing Muggletonians or right-wing Fifth Monarchy Men and to see their founding father as downright odd and perhaps neurotic.

Returning to some of the basic Christian affirmations to be found in Barclay's theology, one of the most important is his constant declaration of differences occasioned by the New Covenant and the era of the Gospel. These emphases need to be compared in detail with Fox, who seems to develop somewhat greater continuity with the Old Testament at a number of points. Yet Fox asserts great discontinuity in regard to ritualization and calendarization, matters on which Barclay is in close agreement. Both see rites ended by the New Covenant and find order (even world order) to be of an altogether different kind. There is also a basic change in the orientation of the individual toward God.

While Fox does not deny the radical changes in values and behavior demanded by Christ, where they do not conflict he manages to hold fast to the ideals of justice, brotherhood, and holiness that are often more sharply etched in the Old Testament. Barclay seems closer to Luther's sharp dichotomy between Law and Gospel, whereas Fox finds a bridge through the prophets, reading them as constantly iterating unsurpassed standards of righteousness and holiness. And through the imagery of a people of God, the prophets are forever calling Israel to unswerving faithfulness.

Certainly in the following quotations Barclay varies little from Fox, if at all, in his understanding of the difference that Christ makes. "The sacrifices which were used by men . . . were all abrogated with the coming of the Son, who is the Substance, eternal Word, and essential Oath and Amen; and in whom the promises of God are Yea and Amen. He came that men might be redeemed from strife, and to bring an end to controversy." *[414]* "As the Just One . . . he suffered for us, the unjust, in order to bring us to God . . . . Through Christ . . . we are given the capability of being reconciled." *[130-131]*

If much of this sounds like the familiar Gospel that has been proclaimed for centuries, it is! There are great areas of commonality that need to be kept in mind when examining the points at which they differ. Some of this has been spelled out as we dealt with the significance of the Gospel for the individual, its implications for the people of God as a whole, their relationship to people of other faiths or none, and (among a number of other things) the critique provided on the right use of the creation.

Most important is the clear confession "that by ourselves we are unable to do anything good. There is no act of our own that will procure remission of sins for us, or oblige God to grant this . . . . Justification arises, instead, from the love of God for us . . . [and] God demonstrated this love for us by sending into the world his beloved Son, the Lord Jesus Christ." *[130]*

Notes to Appendix 2

Italic figures in brackets within the text refer to page numbers in Barclay's *Apology in Modern English*.

1 Cf. *Apology in Modern English*, p. xvii.
2 Cf. "The Early Quakers and The Doctrine of Authority," *Quaker Religious Thought*, vol. 15, no. 1 (Autumn 1973): 4-38; and *The Bible – its Criticism, Interpretation and Use – in 16th and 17th Century England* (Catholic and Quaker Studies, No. 4 available from C & Q. S., 1110 Wildwood Ave., Manasquan, NJ 08736, $8.50 plus $1.50 postage and handling), pp. 97-102: both are by Dean Freiday.

3 In his "'Into That Which Cannot Be Shaken'": The Apocalyptic Gospel Preached by George Fox," in *The Day of the Lord: Eschatology in Quaker Perspective*, ed. by Dean Freiday (Newberg, Ore.: Published at The Barclay Press by The Faith and Life Movement, 1981), pp. 61-96.

Douglas Gwyn's Drew University Ph. D. Thesis (1982, *The Apocalyptic Word of God: The Life and Message of George Fox (1624-1691)*, has additional material on other aspects of Fox's use of Scripture.
4 For some of the content of one of these, written in Latin, cf. my "Barclay's Reply to Arnoldus," *Quaker History*, vol. 68, no. 1 (Spring, 1979): 20–32.
5 The term "Trinity" has been avoided. A chapter has dealt in detail with the attitudes of these authors regarding this doctrine, which most other seventeenth century Christians regarded as sacrosanct, although many Christian theologians today consider the Greek metaphysical terms in which it is stated to be hopelessly outdated.
6 Raimundo Panikkar views the truths behind the doctrine of the Trinity as so vital to Christianity that he uses them as the starting point for dialogue with the World Religions in his *The Trinity and the Religious Experience of Man: Icon–Person–Mystery* (Maryknoll, NY: Orbis, 1973). Nonetheless, he views the "reverential awe" in which the mystery of the Trinity has been held to have "virtually allowed [its] *atrophy* in a great part of Christianity" (p. 6). The modern conception of "person" provides difficulties for the coequality of the Spirit: "The Spirit 'in himself,'" Father Panikkar says, "is a contradiction. There is only the Spirit *of* God, of the Father and Son. He is the One sent. He is neither an I who speaks to another, nor a Thou to whom someone else speaks, but rather the *We* between the Father and the Son . . . there is no room for egoism in the Trinity. It has no *Ding an sich*, selfhood as such." (p. 61.)